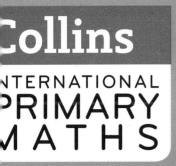

Collins
INTERNATIONAL PRIMARY MATHS

Student's Book 4

William Collins' dream of knowledge for all began with the publication of his first book in 1819.
A self-educated mill worker, he not only enriched millions of lives, but also founded a flourishing publishing house. Today, staying true to this spirit, Collins books are packed with inspiration, innovation and practical expertise. They place you at the centre of a world of possibility and give you exactly what you need to explore it.

Collins. Freedom to teach.

An imprint of HarperCollins*Publishers*
The News Building
1 London Bridge Street
London
SE1 9GF

Browse the complete Collins catalogue at
www.collins.co.uk

10 9 8 7 6 5 4 3 2 1

ISBN 978-0-00-815994-8

Caroline Clissold and Paul Wrangles assert their moral rights to be identified as the authors of this work.

British Library Cataloguing in Publication Data
A catalogue record for this publication is available from the British Library.

Commissioned by Fiona McGlade
Series editor Peter Clarke
Project editor Kate Ellis
Project managed by Emily Hooton
Developed by Tracy Thomas and Karen Williams
Edited by Catherine Dakin
Proofread by Karen Williams
Cover design by Ink Tank
Cover artwork by KPG_Payless/Shutterstock
Internal design by Ken Vail Graphic Design
Typesetting by Ken Vail Graphic Design
Illustrations by Ken Vail Graphic Design, Advocate Art, Beehive Illustration and QBS
Production by Lauren Crisp

Printed and bound by Grafica Veneta S. P. A.

Photo acknowledgements

Every effort has been made to trace copyright holders. Any omission will be rectified at the first opportunity.

Front cover and title page KPG_Payless/Shutterstock

p1 Lester Balajadia/Shutterstock, p5tl Gunter Nezhoda/Shutterstock, p5tr Steve Lovegrove/Shutterstock, p5bl nito/Shutterstock, p5br logoboom/Shutterstock, p13tl Jojoo64/Shutterstock, p13tr Tony Baggett/Shutterstock, p14 Denis Kuvaev/Shutterstock, p15l Luis Carlos Torres/Shutterstock, p15c moprea/Shutterstock, p15r AyalamAdir/Shutterstock, p16r Niloo/Shutterstock, p35 michaeljung/Shutterstock, p36 Andrey Armyagov/Shutterstock, p43l Bojan Pavlukovic/Shutterstock, p43r ruigsantos/Shutterstock, p74 Daniel Wright98/Shutterstock, p75 Adwo/Shutterstock, p76 AVN Photo Lab/Shutterstock, p77 Prasenjeet Gautam /Shutterstock, p78 Restimage/Shutterstock, p79 Lee Yiu Tung/Shutterstock, p80 Pavel L Photo and Video/Shutterstock, p81 Fotonio/Shutterstock, p82 Login/Shutterstock, p83 sandra zuerlein/Shutterstock, p84 Phecsone/Shutterstock, p85 Artisticco/Shutterstock, p86 Honey Cloverz/Shutterstock, p87 NaturePixel/Shutterstock, p88 Manfred Ruckszio/Shutterstock, p89 Andrey_Popov/Shutterstock, p90 Africa Studio/Shutterstock, p91 Duplass/Shutterstock, p92 Lucky Business/Shutterstock, p93 Andrey_Popov/Shutterstock, p94 flashgun/Shutterstock, p95 Veronica Louro/Shutterstock, p96t aimy27feb/Shutterstock, p96b pukach/Shutterstock, p97 Tyler Olson/Shutterstock, p98 Awe Inspiring Images/Shutterstock, p99 kai keisuke/Shutterstock, p100 Andrey_Popov/Shutterstock, p101 Andre Helbig/Shutterstock, p102 Tyler Olson/Shutterstock, p103 Fotofermer/Shutterstock, p104 Destinyweddingstudio/Shutterstock, p105 Henryk Sadura/Shutterstock, p106 Stuart Miles/Shutterstock, p107 Wallenrock/Shutterstock, p108 Hibrida/Shutterstock, p109 Peter Betts/Shutterstock, p110 Goran J/Shutterstock, p111 Petr Malyshev/Shutterstock, p112 NikitaRoytman Photography/Shutterstock, p113 Stephen Rees/Shutterstock.

Contents

Number

1   Whole numbers 1   1
2   Whole numbers 2   5
3   Whole numbers 3   9
4   Decimals 1   13
5   Decimals 2   17
6   Fractions   21
7   Addition and subtraction 1   29
8   Addition and subtraction 2   37
9   Addition and subtraction 3   41
10   Multiplication and division 1   49
11   Multiplication and division 2   57
12   Multiplication and division 3   65

Geometry

13   2D shape, including symmetry   73
14   3D shape   81
15   Position and movement   85

Measure

16 Length   89

17 Mass   93

18 Capacity   97

19 Measures   101

20 Time   105

21 Area and perimeter   109

Handling data

22 Handling data 1   113

23 Handling data 2   117

Number

Lesson 1: **Counting, reading and writing numbers**

- Read and write numbers to 10 000
- Recognise multiples of 5, 10 and 100

Key words
- thousand
- hundred
- digit
- numeral
- multiple

Discover

Numbers can be written in words and numerals. As numbers get larger, it becomes easier and quicker to read them when they are written in numerals.

QUEBEC CITY
727 km

ULAANBAATAR
9824 km

MOSCOW
7492 km

TOKYO
10360 km

RIYADH
10649 km

TAIPEI
12091 km

Learn

Multiples of **5** end in a **0** or a **5**.

5 10 105 100 155 735 505 1000

Multiples of **10** end in a **0**.

10 40 180 390 400 570 1000 2010

Multiples of **100** end in **two zeroes**.

100 300 600 1000 2200 3900 5000

Example

Seven thousand, two hundred and thirty can be written as 7230.

7230 is a multiple of 5 and also 10, but not a multiple of 100.

Lesson 2: **Place value**

* Know the value of each digit in a 4-digit number

Discover

A place value chart can help us to split a 4-digit number into 1000s, 100s, 10s and 1s.

thousands	hundreds	tens	ones
1	4	9	6

Learn

How could this fork be used to teach 4-digit numbers?

What 4-digit number does it show?

The corn on the fork can be written as 2000 + 300 + 10 + 4

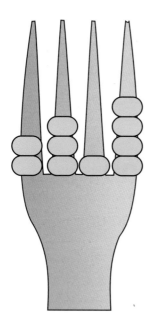

2000 > 300 > 10 > 4

Example

3918 = 3000 + 900 + 10 + 8

2015 = 2000 + 10 + 5

Number

Lesson 3: **Rounding whole numbers**

- Round 3- and 4-digit numbers to the nearest 10 or 100

Key words
- round
- multiple

Discover

What do you notice about the price of the silver car?

$8000 $5550 $2400 $6750 $8426

Learn

The prices of large items like houses or cars are often rounded to the nearest $10 or $100. This makes the prices much easier to remember and to compare.

When rounding to the nearest 10, we look at the units digit only.

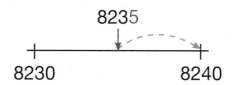

8235

8230   8240

8235 ends in 5, so it is rounded **up** to the nearest 10.

When rounding to the nearest 100, we look at the tens and units digits.

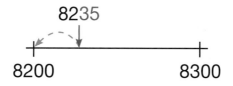

8235

8200   8300

8235 ends in 35, so it is rounded **down** to the nearest 100.

Lesson 4: **Comparing and ordering numbers**

Key words
* more than >
* less than <
* compare
* estimate

* Compare 3- and 4-digit numbers using > and < signs
* Order 3- and 4-digit numbers

Discover

When a number line is used to show different years in order it is called a timeline.

In which order should these years go on the timeline?

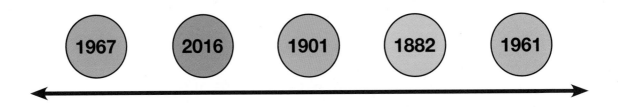

Learn

The > and < symbols can be used to compare numbers.

The narrow part of the symbol always points to the smaller number.

narrow part

3 ˂ 6

3 is less than 6.

9 > 4

9 is more than 4.

Always compare numbers by looking at the digits from left to right.

Example
2016 > 1882 (is more than)
1961 < 1967 (is less than)

Number

Lesson 1: **Multiples of 10, 100, 1000 more and less (1)**

Key words
- thousand
- numeral
- multiple
- sequence

- Find multiples of 10, 100 and 1000 more and less than a number

Discover

We can find examples of 4-digit numbers everywhere!

Where might you see a counter like this?

Learn

The digits from left to right in a 4-digit number are worth 1000s, 100s, 10s and 1s.

If the number increases by 2000, the 1000s digit increases by 2.

$$2143 + 4000 = 6143$$

If the number decreases by 600, the 100s digit decreases by 6.

$$9675 - 600 = 9075$$

Notice how **two digits** change when we cross the 100s boundary.

$$3712 + 90 = 3802$$

5

Number

Lesson 2: **Place value and rounding**

- Know the value of each digit in a 4-digit number
- Round 3- and 4-digit numbers to the nearest 10 or 100

Discover

This target is marked with thousands, hundreds, tens and units.

Why is it easy to calculate the total?

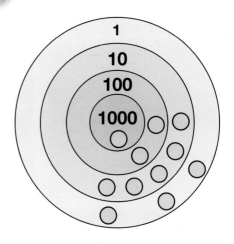

Learn

The position of a digit in a number affects its value.

4-digit numbers are made up of thousands, hundreds, tens and units.

The number 2485 contains 2 thousands (2000), 4 hundreds (400), 8 tens (80) and 5 units (5).

To round to the nearest 100, look at the tens digit.
If it is 5 or more, round up, if it is 4 or less, round down.

Example

rounds down to 3100

Thousands	Hundreds	Tens	Units
3	1	0	4
2	3	7	5

rounds up to 2400

In 3104, the 3 digit is worth 3 thousands.

In 2375, the 3 digit is worth 3 hundreds.

Lesson 3: **Multiplying and dividing by 10 and 100 (1)**

- Multiply and divide numbers by 10 and 100

Key words
- multiply
- divide
- digit
- value

Discover

Place value is important. What two numbers do these digits represent?

Learn

When a number is **multiplied** by 10, its digits shift one place to the **left**.

$75 \times 10 = 750$

When a number is **divided** by 10, its digits shift one place to the **right**.

$640 \div 10 = 64$

If it is **multiplied** by 100, its digits shift two places to the **left**, just like the 3 and the 6 moving up the chairs in the illustration.

To show this, we use zeroes in the empty 10s and 1s places.

$36 \times 100 = 3600$

When a number is **divided** by 100, its digits shift two places to the **right**.

$3600 \div 100 = 36$

Lesson 4: **Odd and even numbers**

Key words
* odd
* even
* sum
* difference

* Recognise odd and even numbers
* Understand what happens to odd and even numbers when they are added or subtracted

Discover

Any number that ends in a 1, 3, 5, 7 or 9 is odd.

Any number that ends in a 2, 4, 6, 8 or 0 is even.

Odd numbers

1733, 2485,

Even numbers

7910, 3742

| 7910 | | 3742 |

| 2485 | | 1733 |

Learn

It is interesting to look at the answers when odd and even numbers are added or subtracted.

Each combination has a different effect on the answer.

Even numbers are multiples of 2.

> **Example**
> ODD + ODD = EVEN
> 35 + 13 = 48
>
> ODD − EVEN = ODD
> 49 − 6 = 43

Number

Lesson 1: **Multiples of 10, 100, 1000 more and less (2)**

• Find multiples of 10, 100 and 1000 more and less than a number

Discover

How far is each jump?
How far does the kangaroo jump in total?

1874   1974   2074   2174   2274

Learn

If you can count in 10s, 100s or 1000s, you can use this to help add or subtract multiples of these numbers.

For example, if you want to find the answer to 5298 + 400, you just need to count forwards in 100s four times.

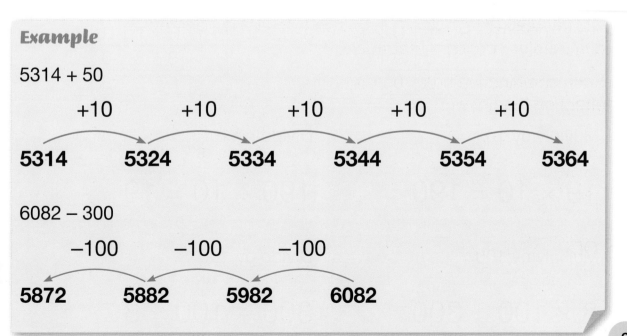

Example

5314 + 50

| +10 | +10 | +10 | +10 | +10 |

5314   5324   5334   5344   5354   5364

6082 − 300

| −100 | −100 | −100 |

5872   5882   5982   6082

9

Lesson 2: **Multiplying and dividing by 10 and 100 (2)**

Number

* Multiply and divide numbers by 10 and 100

Discover

In picture 1, what value does each zero represent? If we added two zeroes to the front of picture 2 would it change the value of the number?

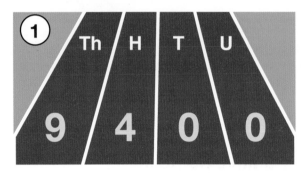

Learn

When a number is multiplied or divided by 10 or 100, its digits don't change, they just move. Empty 10s and units places are filled with zeroes to show there is now nothing there.

19×100

Th	H	T	U
		1	9
1	9	0	0

$380 \div 10$

Th	H	T	U
	3	8	0
		3	8

Multiply by 10

$19 \times 10 = 190$

Multiply by 100

$3 \times 100 = 300$

Divide by 10

$190 \div 10 = 19$

Divide by 100

$300 \div 100 = 3$

Number

Lesson 3: **Negative numbers**

- Use negative numbers correctly in different situations

Discover

Water freezes at 0°C.

How would you show a temperature colder than zero?

Learn

Numbers that are more than zero are called **positive** numbers.

Numbers that are less than zero are called **negative** numbers. These have a minus sign in front of them to show they are less than zero.

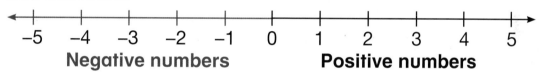

$$-5 \quad -4 \quad -3 \quad -2 \quad -1 \quad 0 \quad 1 \quad 2 \quad 3 \quad 4 \quad 5$$

Negative numbers   **Positive numbers**

Negative numbers are often used to show something below a level, a missing amount or on a scale that shows numbers less than zero.

Example

The submarine is 300 m below sea level. This could be written as −300 m.

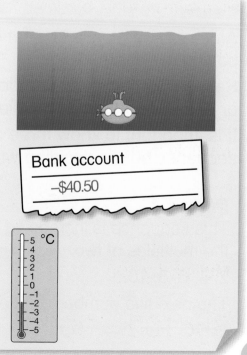

My bank account is showing −$40.50. This means I owe the bank $40.50.

Bank account
−$40.50

The temperature outside is minus 2. This means it is less than zero.

Number

Lesson 4: **Number sequences**

- Recognise different number sequences and extend them

Key words
- **sequence**
- **pattern**
- **increase**
- **decrease**
- **negative**

Discover

Number sequences are all around us. Objects and shapes are often arranged in patterns that get larger or smaller. Many numbers are written in sequences that have a rule.

For example, all the houses on this side of the street increase by two each time.

1   3   5   7   ?   ?

Learn

A number sequence is a set of numbers that follow a particular pattern.

Sequences can show numbers increasing (getting larger) or decreasing (getting smaller).

It is important to know three or four of the numbers in the sequence before deciding what the rule is.

Example

This sequence is increasing by two each time (+2). It also shows the multiples of two.

2, 4, 6, 8, 10…

The next two numbers in the sequence are 12 and 14.

Number

Lesson 1: **Tenths (1)**

- Understand the value of tenths in a number
- Recognise the link between fractions and decimals

📌 **Key words**
- fraction
- decimal
- tenths
- value

Discover

Numbers are not always whole.

Just like fractions, decimals are a way of showing part of a number.

Learn

Tenths are a special way of showing a part of a number.

They can be written as fractions: $\frac{1}{10}$ or $\frac{2}{10}$.

They can also be written as decimals: 0·1 or 0·2.

There are 10 tenths in one whole.

thousands	hundreds	tens	units		tenths
1	4	9	6	·	7

0   0·1   0·2   0·3   0·4   0·5   0·6   0·7   0·8   0·9   1·0

Example

0·2 grams is the same as 0 whole grams and 2 tenths of a gram.

U	·	t	
0	·	2	g

21·5 metres is the same as 21 whole metres and $\frac{5}{10}$ of a metre.

T	U	·	t	
2	1	·	5	m

Lesson 2: **Tenths (2)**

- Understand the value of tenths in a number
- Read and write tenths in different situations

> **Key words**
> - decimal
> - tenths
> - value

Discover

Decimals are all around us because not all numbers are completely whole.

Decimal numbers are used to show parts of numbers.

4·2 m

Learn

Each digit in a number is worth ten times more than the digit to its right.

×10   ×10   ×10

H	T	U	·	t

10 units make one ten. 10 tens make one hundred.

If you split one unit into ten equal pieces, they are each worth one tenth (or $\frac{1}{10}$) or 0·1.

Example

0·1 metres = 0 whole metres and $\frac{1}{10}$ of a metre

4·6 metres = 4 whole metres and $\frac{6}{10}$ of a metre

2·0 metres = 2 whole metres and $\frac{0}{10}$ of a metre.

T	U	·	t
	0	·	1
	4	·	6
	2	·	0

Lesson 3: **Hundredths (1)**

- Understand the value of hundredths in a number
- Recognise the link between fractions and decimals

Number

Discover

Sometimes using tenths is not enough to describe a fraction.

Look carefully at these numbers and compare them with the numbers in Lesson 1.

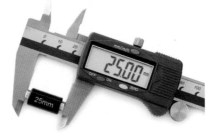

Learn

In the same way that units can be split into 10, tenths can also be split into 10.

These are called **hundredths**.

There are 100 hundredths in one whole.

You can write hundredths as fractions, like $\frac{5}{100}$ or $\frac{83}{100}$.

Or as decimals, like 0.05 or 0.83

| 0 | 0·10 | 0·20 | 0·30 | 0·40 | 0·50 | 0·60 | 0·70 | 0·80 | 0·90 | 1·00 |

Example

U	·	t	h
3	·	0	6

l

3·06 litres = $3 + \frac{6}{100}$

U	·	t	h
1	·	5	2

$

$1·52 = 1 + \frac{5}{10} + \frac{2}{100}$ or $1 + \frac{52}{100}$

T	U	·	t	h
4	0	·	5	0

km

40·50 km = $40 + \frac{50}{100}$ or $40 + \frac{5}{10}$

You can also write this decimal as 40·5 km.

Lesson 4: **Hundredths (2)**

- Understand the value of hundredths in a number
- Read and write hundredths in different situations

Key words
- decimal
- tenths
- hundredths
- value

Discover

One of the most common places we use hundredths in everyday life is when using money.

MENU

$1.15 $1.35

$2.99 $4.99

$2.89

$3.70

$4.09

Learn

Ten 10 cent coins make 1 whole dollar.
Each 10 cent coin is a tenth.

One hundred 1 cent coins make 1 whole dollar.
Each 1 cent coin is a hundredth.

Example

Whole dollars	Tenths of a dollar	Hundredths of a dollar	Amount ($)
1	6	2	$1.62
4	5	0	$4.50

Lesson 1: **Tenths (3)**

- Understand the value of tenths in a number
- Label decimal numbers and order them
- Read and write tenths in different situations

Key words
- decimal
- tenths
- value
- seconds

Number

Discover

We can use decimal numbers to show parts of measurements. These race times show whole numbers of seconds and tenths.

15·3 seconds
16·7 seconds
14·9 seconds
15·9 seconds
14·2 seconds

Learn

One tenth of a number is equal to a unit (one whole) split into ten equal parts.

= 1 whole
= 1

= 1 tenth
= 0·1

This is a way of showing whole numbers with a fraction (or part of a whole) to the right of the decimal point.

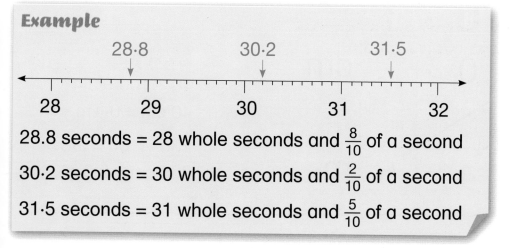

Example

28·8   30·2   31·5

28   29   30   31   32

28.8 seconds = 28 whole seconds and $\frac{8}{10}$ of a second

30·2 seconds = 30 whole seconds and $\frac{2}{10}$ of a second

31·5 seconds = 31 whole seconds and $\frac{5}{10}$ of a second

Lesson 2: **Tenths (4)**

- Understand the value of tenths in a number
- Convert whole centimetres into lengths in metres (in tenths)

Key words
- decimal
- tenths
- metres
- centimetres
- convert

Number

Discover

If you know how many centimetres something is, you can use this to write the measurement in metres as a decimal.

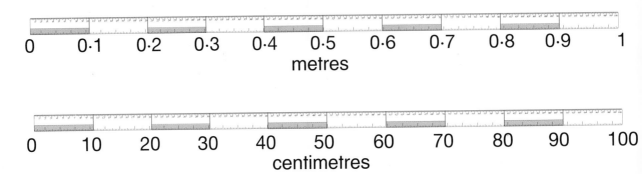

metres

centimetres

Learn

There are 100 centimetres in a metre.

To convert a measurement from centimetres to metres, we divide it by 100.

Each digit moves two places to the right.

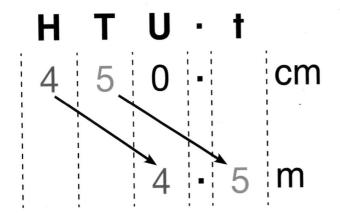

H T U · t

4 5 0 · cm

4 · 5 m

Example

$40 \div 100 = 0 \cdot 4$

$40 \text{ cm} = 0 \cdot 4 \text{ m}$

$230 \div 100 = 2 \cdot 3$

$230 \text{ cm} = 2 \cdot 3 \text{ m}$

Lesson 3: **Hundredths (3)**

- Read, write, label and order hundredths
- Describe and continue decimal number sequences
- Convert prices written in cents into dollars
  (and dollars into cents)

Key words
- decimal
- hundredths
- convert
- dollars
- cents

Number

Discover

Prices can be written in different ways.

$2.50 or 250c

$1.27 or 127c

BARGAINS

$1.99 or 199c

Learn

There are 100 cents in a dollar

To convert a measurement from cents to dollars, we divide it by 100. Each digit moves two places to the right.

$312 \div 100 = 3.12$ 312 cents = $3.12

To convert a measurement from dollars to cents, we multiply it by 100. Each digit moves two places to the left.

$18.50 \times 100 = 1850$

$18.50 = 1850 cents

Example

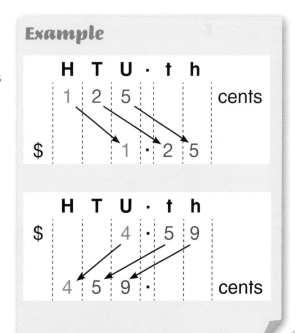

	H	T	U	·	t	h	
	1	2	5				cents
$			1	·	2	5	

	H	T	U	·	t	h	
$			4	·	5	9	
	4	5	9	·			cents

19

Lesson 4: **Hundredths (4)**

- Read, write, order and round decimals in different situations
- Convert measurements using decimals

Key words
- fraction
- decimal
- tenths
- hundredths

Discover

Decimal numbers are a way of showing parts of numbers.

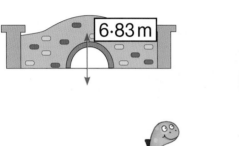

6·83 m

4·34 *l*

9·12 kg

$5.90

2·5 km

Learn

The value of each digit after the decimal point is less than one. One tenth (0·1) is $\frac{1}{10}$ of 1 and one hundredth (0·01) is $\frac{1}{10}$ of 0·1. or $\frac{1}{100}$ of 1.

There are <u>3</u> tenths and <u>6</u> hundredths in the number 6·36.

Like any other number, decimals are read from left to right. Comparing the digits in this way helps us to order them.

These decimals are written in order from smallest to largest.

3·63, 6·33, 6·36, 6·63

Decimals are used in measurements and we can convert from one unit of measurement to another.

6.63 metres is equal to 663 centimetres.

Lesson 1: **Comparing and ordering fractions (1)**

- Compare and order fractions that have the same denominator

Key words
- denominator
- numerator
- compare
- order

Number

Discover

If fractions have the same **denominator** it is easy to compare them.

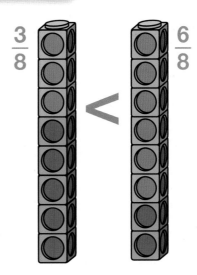

$\frac{3}{8} < \frac{6}{8}$

Learn

The **denominator** in a fraction is the bottom number. This shows the number of parts something has been divided into.

The **numerator** in a fraction is the top number. This shows the number being considered.

When fractions have the same bottom number, you just need to compare the top numbers to see which is larger or smaller.

Example

3 is larger than 1.
So $\frac{3}{4}$ is larger than $\frac{1}{4}$.

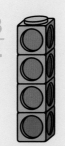 $\frac{3}{4}$

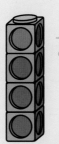 $\frac{1}{4}$

21

Number

Lesson 2: **Equivalent fractions**

Key words
• **equivalent**
• **numerator**
• **denominator**

- Identify fractions that are equal to $\frac{1}{2}$, $\frac{1}{4}$ and $\frac{1}{5}$

Discover

Some fractions are worth the same amount, even though they are written differently.

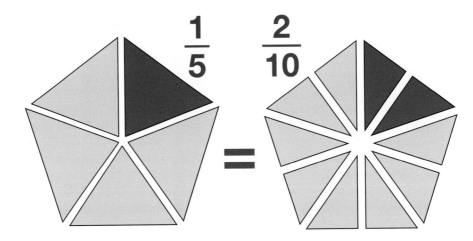

$$\frac{1}{5} \quad \frac{2}{10}$$

Learn

Equivalent fractions are fractions that look different but have the same value. They have different numbers and have been divided into a different number of parts, but they are worth the same.

In the Discover diagram, the second shape has been split into twice as many parts as the first shape. The parts are half the size, so you need two of them to equal one part in the first shape. So $\frac{1}{5}$ is the same as $\frac{2}{10}$.

A useful way to find equivalent fractions is to use a fraction wall, or fraction strips.

Example

$$\frac{1}{4} = \frac{2}{8}$$

Number

Lesson 3: **Comparing and ordering fractions (2)**

- Compare and order fractions that have different denominators

Discover

Even though some fractions may have different denominators, we can still compare them.

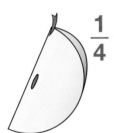

$\frac{1}{4}$

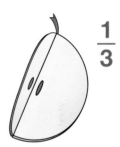

$\frac{1}{3}$

Quarter of an apple

Third of an apple

Learn

When fractions have different denominators, they can be made easier to compare by working out what they are equivalent to.

To compare $\frac{3}{4}$ and $\frac{3}{8}$, we can see if they are equivalent to a half.

$\frac{3}{4}$ is more than a half (or $\frac{2}{4}$).

A half is also $\frac{4}{8}$, so $\frac{3}{8}$ is less than a half. Therefore $\frac{3}{4}$ is greater than $\frac{3}{8}$.

$\frac{4}{10}$ is less than $\frac{3}{5}$ because $\frac{3}{5}$ in tenths is $\frac{6}{10}$ and $\frac{4}{10}$ is less than $\frac{6}{10}$.

Example

Write these fractions in order: $\frac{2}{4}$, $\frac{9}{10}$, $\frac{1}{5}$ $\frac{1}{5}$, $\frac{2}{4}$, $\frac{9}{10}$

This is because $\frac{1}{5}$ is less than a half (in tenths, $\frac{1}{5}$ is worth $\frac{2}{10}$),

$\frac{2}{4}$ equals a half ($\frac{1}{2}$ in tenths is worth $\frac{5}{10}$) and $\frac{9}{10}$ is more than a half.

Lesson 4: **Equivalent fractions and decimals (1)**

• Identify fractions and decimal numbers that are equivalent

Discover

Fractions and decimals can show equal amounts.

$\frac{1}{10}$	$\frac{1}{10}$	$\frac{1}{10}$	$\frac{1}{10}$	$\frac{1}{10}$
$\frac{1}{10}$	$\frac{1}{10}$	$\frac{1}{10}$	$\frac{1}{10}$	$\frac{1}{10}$

=

0·1	0·1	0·1	0·1	0·1
0·1	0·1	0·1	0·1	0·1

Learn

The places to the right of the decimal point in a number are worth tenths and hundredths.

Units	·	Tenths	Hundredths
0	·	2	0

This means decimals can be written as fractions that are equivalent:

0·2 has 2 in the tenths place.

So, 0·2 is equal, or equivalent, to $\frac{2}{10}$

Example

$0·6 = \frac{6}{10}$

Units	·	Tenths	Hundredths
0	·	6	0

$0·04 = \frac{4}{100}$

Units	·	Tenths	Hundredths
0	·	0	4

$0·08 = \frac{8}{100}$

Units	·	Tenths	Hundredths
0	·	0	8

Lesson 5: **Equivalent fractions and decimals (2)**

Key words
• decimal
• equivalent
• tenths
• hundredths

- Identify fractions and decimal numbers that are equivalent

Discover

Fractions can be written using decimal numbers.

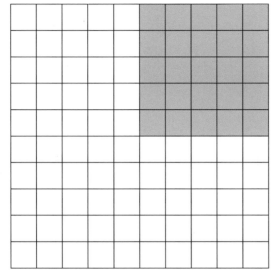

$\dfrac{25}{100}$

$\dfrac{1}{4} = 0.25$

Learn

Even though many fractions are not tenths or hundredths, you can still write them as decimals.

One way to do this is to think of equivalent fractions that are in tenths or hundredths and use these to help.

The square above shows that 25 is one quarter of 100, so $\frac{1}{4}$ is equivalent to $\frac{25}{100}$.

Once you know this, you can write the decimal for $\frac{1}{4}$ as 0.25.

Example

$\frac{5}{10}$ is equivalent to $\frac{1}{2}$, so you write $\frac{1}{2}$ as a decimal as 0.5.

$\frac{1}{2} = \frac{5}{10}$ (or $\frac{50}{100}$) = 0.5 (or 0.50)

Lesson 6: **Mixed numbers**

- Recognise mixed numbers
- Put mixed numbers in the correct order on a number line

Key words
- mixed number
- whole number
- fraction
- order

Number

Discover

Mixed numbers show a whole amount as well as a fraction.

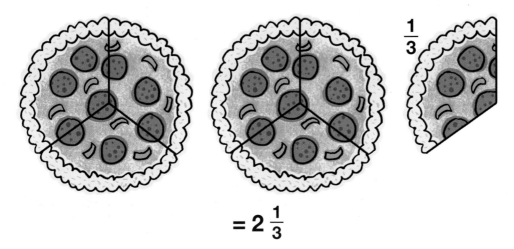

$$= 2\frac{1}{3}$$

Learn

A mixed number is a number that is made up of a whole number and a fraction.

You can put mixed numbers in order on a number line by first comparing the whole number and then the fraction.

Example

$4\frac{3}{4}$ belongs in between 4 and 5 on a number line, $\frac{3}{4}$ of the way along.

Lesson 7: **Relating fractions to division**

• Recognise links between fractions and division
• Say the division needed to work out a fraction calculation

Key words
• divide
• numerator
• denominator

Discover

If you know how to divide, you can find fractions of numbers and shapes.

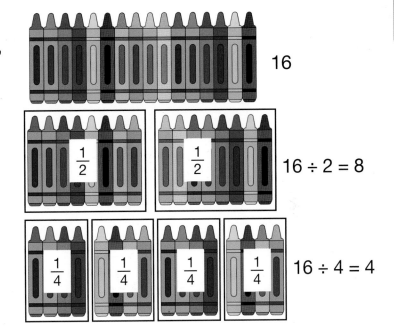

16

$16 \div 2 = 8$

$16 \div 4 = 4$

Learn

Finding a fraction of a number is the same as dividing that number. For example, finding $\frac{1}{4}$ is the same as dividing by 4.

You can use this information to find more complicated fractions. If you know what one quarter is worth, you can use this to work out what three quarters are worth.

$$\frac{1}{4} \text{ of } 16 = 4 \qquad \frac{3}{4} \text{ of } 16 = 4 \times 3 = 12$$

Example

$$\frac{1}{8} \text{ of } 32 = 32 \div 8$$
$$= 4$$

$$\frac{1}{5} \text{ of } 45 = 45 \div 5$$
$$= 9$$

Lesson 8: **Finding fractions of shapes and numbers**

Key words
• divide
• numerator
• denominator

• Find halves, quarters, thirds, fifths, eighths and tenths of shapes and numbers

Discover

Shapes and numbers can be split into different fractions as long as each part is the same size.

Learn

When finding a fraction of a shape, you can think of each fraction as showing a part out of a whole. So $\frac{1}{10}$ of a shape is 1 out of a total of 10 equal-sized pieces.

Example

What fraction of this shape is green?

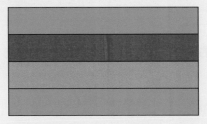

There are four equal stripes, so the shape is split into quarters.

Two out of a total of four are green, so $\frac{2}{4}$ are green.

This is the same as $\frac{1}{2}$.

When finding a fraction of a number, you can use division.

For example, $\frac{1}{10}$ of 40 is found by dividing 40 by 10.

What is $\frac{1}{5}$ of 20? $20 \div 5 = 4$, so $\frac{1}{5}$ of 20 is 4.

Lesson 1: **Adding three or four single-digit numbers**

Key words
• add
• total
• pairs
• complements

- Add three or four single-digit numbers accurately
- Spot pairs of numbers that make addition quicker

Discover

To add several small numbers quickly, it is helpful to look for pairs or groups of numbers that complement each other.

$$8 + 5 + 1 + 4$$

$$6 + 4 + 5 + 3$$

Learn

You already know about addition number bonds to 20. The word **complement** can be used to describe pairs or groups of numbers that go well together because they can be combined to make mental addition easier.

For example, 8 and 2 can be combined to make 10.

Spotting pairs of numbers like these can help you add more quickly.

Example
What is the total of 6, 2, 1 and 4?

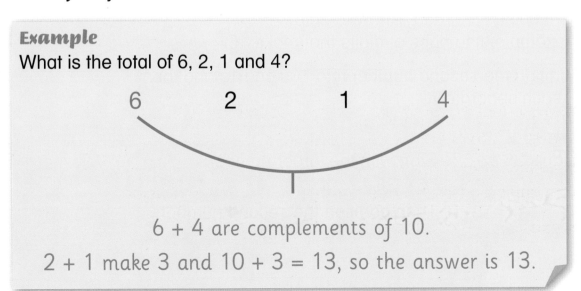

6 + 4 are complements of 10.
2 + 1 make 3 and 10 + 3 = 13, so the answer is 13.

Lesson 2: **Adding pairs of 2-digit numbers**

Key words
- add
- total
- tens
- units
- partition

- Add pairs of 2-digit numbers
- Choose useful strategies to help add numbers

Discover

We can use different strategies to add pairs of 2-digit numbers.

28 + 72

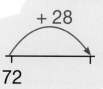

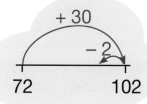

Learn

There are several different strategies you can use to add a pair of 2-digit numbers.

1 Put the larger number first. This makes the calculation easier.

2 Use facts you already know to help.
For example, find pairs of digits that make 10.

3 Partition the second number into 10s and 1s and then add each separately.

> **Example**
> What is 38 + 75? Start with the larger number:
> 75 + 38
> Then partition the second number:
> 75 + 38 = 75 + 30 + 8
> = 105 + 8
> = 113

Lesson 3: **Adding pairs of 3-digit numbers (1)**

Key words
- add
- total
- sum

- Use jottings to help add pairs of 3-digit numbers

Discover

You can use different strategies to find the total of a pair of 3-digit numbers.

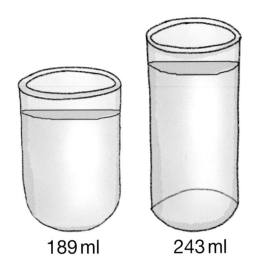

189 ml   243 ml

Learn

When numbers in calculations become larger, they start to become more difficult to solve mentally.

Using a pencil and paper to jot things down, or using an empty number line, can be helpful.

Example
727 + 245

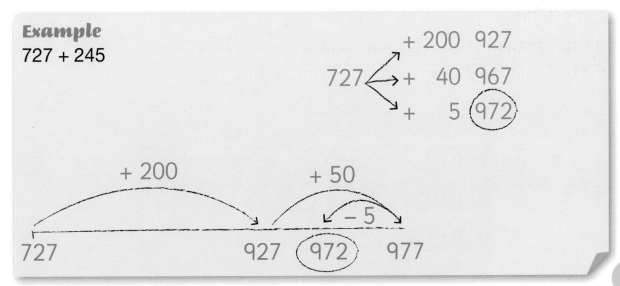

Lesson 4: **Adding pairs of 3-digit numbers (2)**

- Use partitioning to help add pairs of 3-digit numbers

Key words
- add
- total
- sum
- partition

Discover

One way to add a pair of 3-digit numbers is to split them into smaller parts.

| 3 | 5 | 6 |

| 3 | 0 | 0 | | 5 | 0 | | 6 |

| 4 | 7 | 7 |

| 4 | 0 | 0 | | 7 | 0 | | 7 |

Learn

3-digit numbers can be partitioned (or split up) into hundreds, tens and units to make it easier to add them.

You can find the totals of the hundreds, the tens and the units, before adding them to find the overall total.

Example

735 + 246 = | 7 | 0 | 0 | + | 2 | 0 | 0 | + | 3 | 0 | + | 4 | 0 | + | 5 | + | 6 |

= | 9 | 0 | 0 | + | 7 | 0 | + | 1 | 1 |

= | 9 | 8 | 1 |

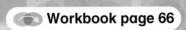

Lesson 5: **Subtracting pairs of 2-digit numbers**

Number

• Subtract pairs of 2-digit numbers
• Choose useful strategies to help subtract numbers

Discover

You can use different strategies to subtract 2-digit numbers.

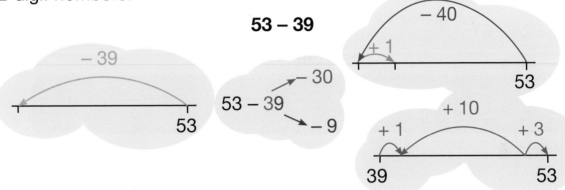

53 − 39

Learn

There are several different strategies you can use to subtract a pair of 2-digit numbers.

1 Use facts you already know to help. For example, if the number you are subtracting is a near multiple of 10, take the multiple of 10 away and then adjust the answer.

2 Instead of counting back, start with the smaller number and count on until you reach the larger number. This strategy works well when the numbers are close together.

3 Partition the second number into tens and units and then subtract each separately.

Example

What is 85 − 79?

Count on from 79 to 85. This is 6, so 85 − 79 = 6.

33

Number

Lesson 6: **Subtracting a 2-digit number from a 3-digit number**

Key words
* subtract
* difference
* take away
* empty number line

* Use jottings to help subtract 2-digit numbers from 3-digit numbers

Discover

Jotting your ideas down can help when you are subtracting numbers.

824 – 67

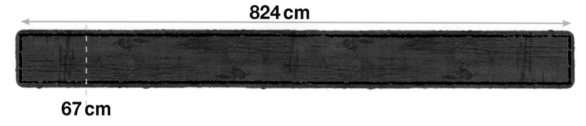

824 cm

67 cm

Learn

It can be difficult to hold the numbers in your head when subtracting 2-digit numbers from 3-digit numbers. One way to help is to use jottings or an empty number line.

Example

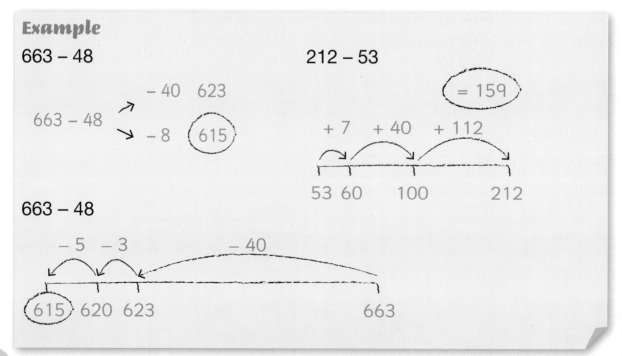

663 – 48

663 – 48
    – 40   623
    – 8   (615)

212 – 53

= 159

+ 7   + 40   + 112

53 60   100   212

663 – 48

– 5 – 3   – 40

(615) 620 623   663

Lesson 7: **Subtracting pairs of 3-digit numbers (1)**

- Use jottings to help subtract pairs of 3-digit numbers

Key words
- subtract
- difference
- take away

Number

Discover

You can subtract a pair of 3-digit numbers by using an empty number line.

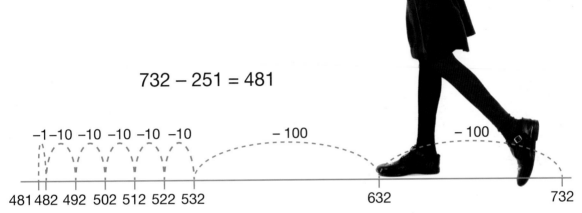

$$732 - 251 = 481$$

Learn

Sketching a blank number line can help when subtracting 3-digit numbers as it allows you to remember the changing answer as the hundreds, tens and units are taken away.

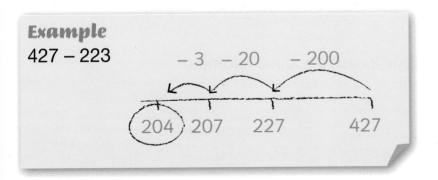

Example
427 − 223

− 3   − 20   − 200

204   207   227   427

Lesson 8: **Subtracting pairs of 3-digit numbers (2)**

- Use jottings to help subtract pairs of 3-digit numbers

Discover

One way to find the difference between two 3-digit numbers is to start with the smaller number and count on.

Day 178 of a year-long mission. How many days left?

$$+2 \quad +20 \quad +165 \quad = 187 \text{ days left}$$
$$178 \quad 180 \quad 200 \quad 365$$

Learn

You can think of subtraction as finding the difference between two numbers.

If you start with the smaller number and count on until you reach the larger number, the number that you have added is the difference.

This is an interesting strategy to use because it turns a subtraction into an addition!

Example

If it is the 284th day of the year, how long is left until the end of the year?

Count on from 284 to 365.

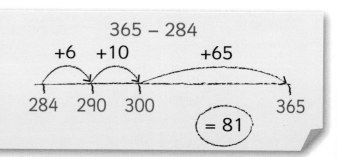

$$365 - 284$$
$$+6 \quad +10 \quad \qquad +65$$
$$284 \quad 290 \quad 300 \qquad\qquad 365$$
$$= 81$$

Lesson 1: **Mental addition (1)**

• Choose useful mental strategies to add numbers

📌 **Key words**
• add
• altogether
• total
• sum of
• increase

Number

Discover

There are lots of different strategies that you can use to add numbers in your head.

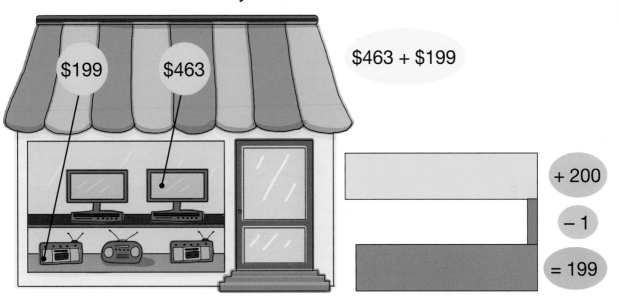

$463 + $199

+ 200

− 1

= 199

Learn

An effective mental strategy is to use an addition fact you already know to help you to find a fact you do not know.

Example

What is 50 + 20 + 60?

I know that 5 + 6 make 11, so 50 + 60 must make 110. If I add the 20, I get 130.

What is the total of 429 and 298?

298 is a near multiple of 100 (it is 2 less than 300). I know that 429 + 300 makes 729 and two less than this number equals 727.

What would you add to 650 to get 1000?

I know that 65 + 35 = 100, so 650 + 350 must equal 1000.

Number

Lesson 2: **Adding pairs of 3-digit numbers (3)**

- Use written methods to add pairs of 3-digit numbers

Discover

3-digit numbers can be added using written methods.

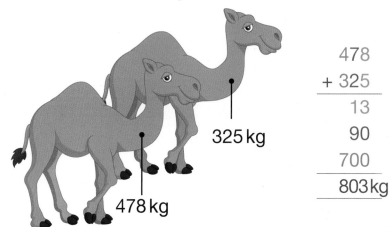

325 kg

478 kg

$$
\begin{array}{r}
478 \\
+\ 325 \\
\hline
13 \\
90 \\
700 \\
\hline
803\,\text{kg} \\
\hline
\end{array}
$$

Learn

You can use written methods to add 3-digit numbers.

First, write both numbers vertically, taking care to keep the units, tens and hundreds on top of each other.

Add the units and write the total underneath.

Then, add the tens and write the total underneath that.

Finally, add the hundreds and write the total underneath that.

To find the overall answer, add all three totals.

Example

What is the total of 578 and 317?

$$
\begin{array}{r}
578 \\
+\ 317 \\
\hline
15 \\
80 \\
800 \\
\hline
895 \\
\hline
\end{array}
$$

◄ the total of the units
◄ the total of the tens
◄ the total of the hundreds

Lesson 3: **Mental subtraction (1)**

- Choose useful mental strategies to subtract numbers

Key words
- subtract
- difference
- take away
- less than
- decrease

Number

Discover

You can choose different mental strategies to find the answer.

$603 – $7

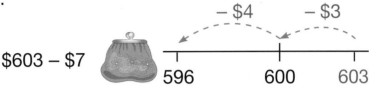

Learn

There is often a strategy that you can use to help.

You can split the smaller number first and then subtract each number separately.

What is 704 – 9?

> I know that 9 can be split into 4 and 5. If I take the 4 away first, it takes me to 700. Then I take the 5 away to get 695.

You can subtract a near number and then adjust the answer.

What is 39 less than 357?

> The number 39 is near to 40, so I can subtract 40 from 357 to get 317. Then I add 1 to adjust the answer to 318.

If the two numbers are close together, you can start with the smaller number and count on.

What is the difference between 402 and 397?

> These numbers are close together, so it is quicker to start with the lower number and count on. 397 plus 3 makes 400 and then I add another 2 to get to 402. The difference is 3 + 2 which equals 5.

Number

Lesson 4: **Subtraction involving 3-digit numbers**

- Use jottings to subtract from 3-digit numbers

Discover

Part of the skill of using different strategies to subtract numbers is to know when to use each strategy. It is just as important to know when **not** to use them too!

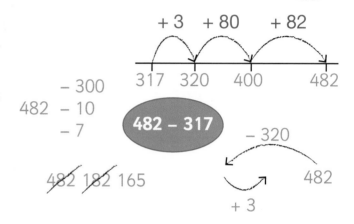

Learn

It is important to choose a strategy that is efficient and reliable when subtracting numbers.

For example:

364 − 146 = ?

Count out 364 cubes. Then count 146 cubes and remove them. Then count the number of cubes which remain.

Is this an efficient strategy? What would be a more efficient way?

Example

358 − 342 These numbers are close to each other, so the quickest way to find the answer is by counting on from the smaller number to the larger.

689 − 21 Counting on from the smaller number in this calculation would not be a good strategy to use as it would take longer than just subtracting 21.

538 − 298 The second number is very close to 300, so a quick strategy would be to subtract 300 and then adjust the answer by adding 2.

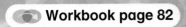

Lesson 1: **Mental addition (2)**

• Choose appropriate mental strategies to add numbers

Discover

Knowing simple addition facts can help you answer more complicated addition questions.

$$4 + 6 = 10$$

$$41 + \boxed{} = 100 \rightarrow 40 + 60 = 100 \leftarrow 450 + \boxed{} = 1000$$

$$500 + 500 = 1000$$

$$400 + 600 = 1000$$

$$7 + 3 = 10$$
$$70 + 30 = 100$$

$$\text{double } 7 = 14 \rightarrow 40 + 70 + 30$$

$$4 + 7 + 3 = 14$$

Learn

Knowing basic addition facts to make 10 can be very helpful when answering more difficult questions.

They are like building blocks that you can use to base more complicated calculations on.

Example

What is 60 + 90 + 40?

> I know that 6 and 4 make 10, so 60 + 40 must make 100. If I add the 90, it makes 190.

What would you add to 68 to get 100?

> If I add 2 to 68, it makes 70. 7 + 3 makes 10, so 70 + 30 makes 100. The answer is 30 plus the 2 I added which equals 32.

What is the total of 723 and 198?

> 198 is two less than 200. 723 plus 200 makes 923 and if I adjust the answer by taking away 2, it equals 921.

Number

Lesson 2: **Mental addition (3)**

- Choose appropriate mental strategies to add pairs of 2-digit numbers
- Identify simple fractions with a total of 1

Key words
- total
- fraction
- whole
- numerator
- denominator

Discover

Some fractions make one whole when they are added together.

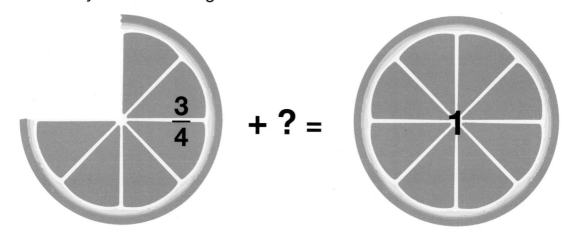

$$\frac{3}{4} + ? = 1$$

Learn

If one whole is split into thirds, this means that there are three equal pieces.

So, you can say that three thirds equal one whole ($\frac{3}{3} = 1$).

In the same way, four quarters equal one whole, and so on.

Knowing facts like this can help you work out what to add to simple fractions to equal 1.

Example

$\frac{1}{3} + \boxed{} = 1$

There are three thirds in one whole, so $\frac{1}{3} + \frac{2}{3} = 1$.

$\frac{4}{5} + \boxed{} = 1$

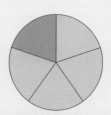

There are five fifths in one whole, so $\frac{4}{5} + \frac{1}{5} = 1$.

Lesson 3: **Adding pairs of 3-digit numbers (4)**

* Use written methods to add pairs of 3-digit numbers

Key words
* column
* vertical
* hundreds
* tens
* units
* written method

Number

Discover

This written method can be used to add 3-digit numbers.

443 m

```
  136
+ 443
─────
    9
   70
  500
─────
  579 m
```

136 m

Learn

By writing 3-digit numbers vertically, you can add the units, tens and hundreds quickly.

There is an even quicker written method if you write down the totals of each column straight away.

Example

What is 628 + 252?

```
  628          628
+ 252        + 252
─────        ─────
   10          880
   70           1
  800
─────
  880
─────
```

43

Number

Lesson 4: **Adding pairs of 3-digit numbers (5)**

- Use written methods to add pairs of 3-digit numbers

Discover

3-digit numbers can be added quickly if they are written vertically in columns.

$$\begin{array}{r} 834 \\ + 473 \\ \hline 1307 \\ \scriptstyle 1 \end{array}$$

Learn

The reason you add the units first, then the tens and finally the hundreds with the vertical written method is because sometimes the total of a column is greater than nine units.

When this happens, it affects the total of the next place value column to the left.

In the Example, 2 tens (20) plus 9 tens (90) makes 11 tens (110).

So, you 'carry' the 1 hundred over to the hundreds column, writing a small 1, and write 1 in the tens column (because 1 ten and 1 hundred make 110).

Example

$$528 + 391 \qquad \begin{array}{r} 528 \\ + 391 \\ \hline 919 \\ \scriptstyle 1 \end{array}$$

44

Lesson 5: **Mental subtraction (2)**

• Choose appropriate mental strategies to subtract numbers

Key words
• subtract
• difference
• hundreds boundary
• strategy
• number fact

Number

Discover

When numbers in a calculation are close to 10 or 100, it makes them easier to add or subtract.

924 – 199　　701 – 695　　878 – 31　　577 – 59　　683 – 298

Learn

To make a subtraction easier, you can round one of the numbers to the nearest 10 or 100, as long as you remember to adjust the answer afterwards!

Another strategy is to spot links between numbers that are close to a hundreds boundary.

Example

What is 796 – 59?

59 is a near multiple of 10. I know that 796 – 60 equals 736 and so I need to adjust the answer by adding 1 to get 737.

What is 503 – 496?

Both numbers are near to the hundreds boundary. I can add 4 to 496 to make 500. 500 add 3 makes 503. 4 + 3 equals 7, so the difference between the two numbers is 7.

Lesson 6: **Mental subtraction (3)**

Number

- Choose appropriate mental strategies to subtract numbers

Key words
- difference
- strategy
- hundreds boundary

Discover

Mental strategies are usually much quicker to use than written ones.

29 kg   4 kg   51 kg   601 kg

Learn

To decide which strategy to use, look at the numbers and try to spot patterns and properties that will help.

You can split numbers into parts, count on or imagine what a subtraction looks like on a number line.

Example

What is 503 − 9?

9 can be split into 3 and 6. Subtract the 3 first, to get to to 500, then subtract the 6 to find the answer, 494.

What is 66 subtracted from 74?

These numbers are close together, so I can count up from the smaller number to the larger. 66 + 4 equals 70 and 70 + 4 equals 74, so the answer is 8.

What is the difference between 631 and 46?

Instead of subtracting 46 straight away I can subtract 40 and then 6. 631 − 40 is 591 and 591 − 6 equals 585.

Number

Lesson 7: **Subtracting pairs of 3-digit numbers (1)**

- Use written methods to subtract pairs of 3-digit numbers

Discover

3-digit numbers can be subtracted using written methods.

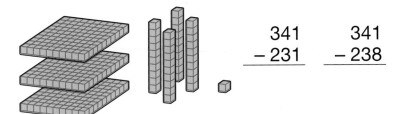

$$\begin{array}{r} 341 \\ -231 \\ \hline \end{array} \qquad \begin{array}{r} 341 \\ -238 \\ \hline \end{array}$$

Learn

The written method for subtraction is similar to the one for addition, except the larger number must always be on the top.

Look at the units column in the second Discover subtraction. When subtracting the units, tens and hundreds, sometimes a digit will be larger on the bottom.

When this happens, the top number needs to be regrouped. It still equals the same amount, but it has been organised in a different way.

Example

$$\begin{array}{r} 341 \\ -238 \\ \hline \end{array}$$

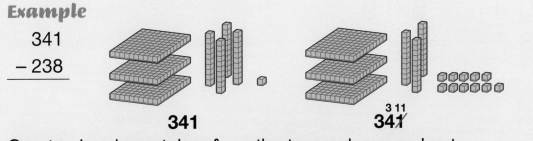

341   **341̸** (3 11)

One ten has been taken from the tens column and put with the units. The top number still adds up to 341, but it has been regrouped. Now we can work out each column.

$$\begin{array}{r} \overset{3\ 11}{34\cancel{1}} \\ -238 \\ \hline 103 \end{array}$$

47

Number

Lesson 8: **Subtracting pairs of 3-digit numbers (2)**

- Use written methods to subtract pairs of 3-digit numbers

Discover

This written method is a way to subtract larger numbers easily.

973 people

427 people

How many people are left?

$$
\begin{array}{r}
\overset{6\ \ 13}{9\cancel{7}3} \\
-\ 427 \\
\hline
546
\end{array}
$$

Learn

By writing a 3-digit subtraction vertically, you can subtract the units, tens and hundreds quickly.

It is important to regroup the top number if any of the columns have a smaller digit on the top than the bottom.

For example:

$$
\begin{array}{r}
5\ 0\ 9 \\
-\ 1\ 8\ 7 \\
\hline
\end{array}
\qquad
\begin{array}{r}
\overset{4\ \ 10}{\cancel{5}\,\cancel{0}\,9} \\
-\ 1\ 8\ 7 \\
\hline
\end{array}
$$

Example

What is 490 – 347?

$$
\begin{array}{r}
\overset{\ \ 8\ 10}{4\,\cancel{9}\,\cancel{0}} \\
-\ 3\ 4\ 7 \\
\hline
1\ 4\ 3
\end{array}
$$

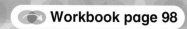

Lesson 1: **Multiplication and division facts (1)**

- Know multiplication and division facts for 2×, 3×, 4×, 5×, 6×, 9× and 10× tables
- Recognise multiples of 2, 3, 4, 5 and 10

Key words
- multiply
- times
- times-tables
- divide
- multiple

Number

Discover

Being able to recall multiplication and division facts is an important maths skill.

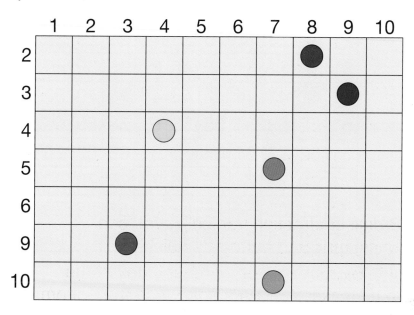

Learn

If you know a multiplication fact, you can use it to help remember division facts.

For example, if you know that 6 lots of 10 make 60, then you also know that 60 divided by 6 equals 60.

Example

3 × 8 = 24	So, 24 ÷ 3 = 8
10 × 7 = 70	So, 70 ÷ 10 = 7
5 × 6 = 30	So, 30 ÷ 5 = 6

Lesson 2: **6× and 9× multiplication and division facts**

Number

* Know multiplication and division facts for 6× and 9× tables

Key words
* **multiply**
* **times**
* **divide**
* **multiple**

Discover

3× tables facts help with both the 6× tables and the 9× tables.

1	2	3	4	5	6	7	8	9	10
11	12	13	14	15	16	17	18	19	20
21	22	23	24	25	26	27	28	29	30
31	32	33	34	35	36	37	38	39	40
41	42	43	44	45	46	47	48	49	50
51	52	53	54	55	56	57	58	59	60
61	62	63	64	65	66	67	68	69	70
71	72	73	74	75	76	77	78	79	80
81	82	83	84	85	86	87	88	89	90
91	92	93	94	95	96	97	98	99	100

Learn

6 and 9 are both multiples of 3, so every number in the 6× and the 9× tables are also in the 3× table.

Work out 6× tables facts by doubling 3× tables facts.

One way of working out 9× tables facts is by multiplying by 10 and then subtracting one lot of the number.

Example

What is 7 times 6?

$7 \times 3 = 21$ and 21 doubled is 42, so $7 \times 6 = 42$.

What is the product of 8 and 9?

$8 \times 10 = 80$ and $80 - 8$ is 72, so $8 \times 9 = 72$.

Lesson 3: **7× and 8× multiplication and division facts**

Key words
* array
* multiply
* times
* divide
* multiple

Number

* Know multiplication and division facts for 7× and 8× tables
* Find the easier way to multiply by reversing multiplications

Discover

There are lots of ways to help us remember all of the times-tables facts.

●●●●●○○
●●●●●○○   (3 × 5) + (3 × 2)
●●●●●○○   = 3 × 7

●●●●●●●●⊘⊘
●●●●●●●●⊘⊘   (3 × 10) − (3 × 2)
●●●●●●●●⊘⊘   = 3 × 8

Learn

If you know your 5× and 4× tables facts, you can use them to help find 7× and 8× tables facts.

5 + 2 makes 7, so you can work out 7× tables facts by working out 5× a number and adding it to 2× the same number.

8 is double 4, so a quick way to work out 8× tables facts is to work out the number multiplied by 4 and then double the answer.

Example

What are 4 lots of 7?

What is 6 multiplied by 8?

4 × 5 = 20
4 × 2 = 8
20 + 8 = 28,
so 4 × 7 = 28

6 × 4 = 24
24 doubled = 48,
so 6 × 8 = 48

Number

Lesson 4: **Multiplying multiples of 10 to 90**

Key words
* **multiply**
* **multiple**

* Multiply multiples of 10 up to 90 by a single-digit number

Discover

You can use facts you already know to help multiply a multiple of 10 by a single-digit number.

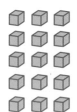

$5 \times 3 = 15$

$50 \times 3 = ?$

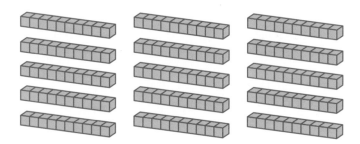

Learn

You can multiply multiples of 10 up to 90 by using facts you already know.

You know that 60×4 is the same as the answer to 6×4 multiplied by 10.

6 times 4 is 24, so 60 times 4 is ten times 24, which equals 240.

Example

What is 50 times 4?

What is 30 multiplied by 9?

$5 \times 4 = 20$,
so $50 \times 4 = 200$

$3 \times 9 = 27$,
so $30 \times 9 = 270$

Lesson 5: **Multiplying a 2-digit number (1)**

- Use partitioning to multiply a 2-digit number by a single-digit number

Key words
- multiply
- partition
- tens
- units
- total

Number

Discover

You can multiply 2-digit numbers by single-digit numbers by partitioning them.

Walking to school
Time taken: 26 min
Number of days: 5
Total time (min): ?

Learn

2-digit numbers can be partitioned (split) into tens and units. For example, the number 53 can be partitioned into 50 and 3.

So, the calculation 53 × 4 can be worked out by calculating 50 × 4, then 3 × 4 and then adding the two answers together.

Example

What is 53 × 4?

$53 \times 4 = (50 \times 4) + (3 \times 4)$

$\qquad = 200 + 12$

$\qquad = 212$

What is the product of 64 and 6?

$64 \times 6 = (60 \times 6) + (4 \times 6)$

$\qquad = 360 + 24$

$\qquad = 384$

Lesson 6: **Multiplying a 2-digit number (2)**

- Use the grid method to multiply a 2-digit number by a single-digit number

Key words
- **multiply**
- **grid method**
- **partition**
- **total**

Discover

We can use a grid to help us to multiply a
2-digit number by a single-digit number.

Games won: 24
Points for a win: 3
Total points:

×	20	4
3	60	12

60 + 12 = 72

Learn

The **grid method** is a way of multiplying larger numbers. You partition
the numbers, multiply them and then add the answers together.

What is 45 × 2?

1 Draw a grid with two columns and one row (because
you are multiplying a 2-digit number by a 1-digit number).

2 Partition the 2-digit number and write the tens and
units across the top and the single-digit down the side.

×	40	5
2		

3 Multiply each number by the single-digit
and write the answers in the grid.

×	40	5
2	80	10

4 Add the answers together to find the total.
80 + 10 = 90, so 45 × 2 = 90.

Example
What is 89 × 4?

×	80	9
4	320	36

320 + 36 = 356, so 89 × 4 = 356.

Lesson 7: **Dividing a 2-digit number (1)**

Key words
• divide
• estimate

• Divide a 2-digit number by a single-digit number

Discover

You can divide a 2-digit number by a single-digit number by breaking the larger number into chunks that you know already.

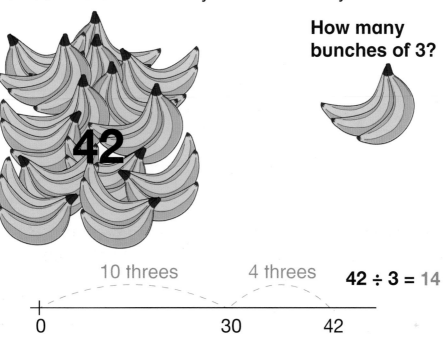

How many bunches of 3?

10 threes   4 threes   **42 ÷ 3 = 14**

0   30   42

Learn

A quick way to divide 2-digit numbers by single-digit numbers is to split them up into larger chunks that you know already.

In the Discover picture, if you know that ten 3s make 30, you only need to count from 30 to 42 in 3s to find the answer.

Example

How many 6s are in 78?

78 ÷ 6 = 13

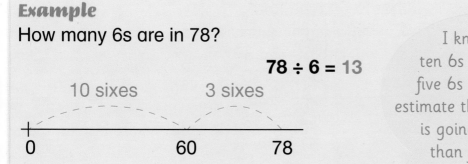

10 sixes   3 sixes

0   60   78

I know that ten 6s are 60 and five 6s are 30, so I estimate that the answer is going to be less than fifteen 6s.

Lesson 8: **Dividing a 2-digit number (2)**

Key words
- divide
- estimate
- inverse function

• Divide a 2-digit number by a single-digit number

Discover

Multiplication facts can help us answer division questions.

90 eggs. 6 per box. How many boxes?

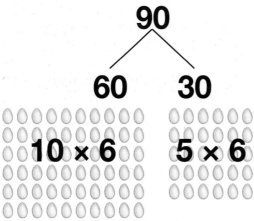

Learn

You can use multiplication facts you already know to divide a 2-digit number by a single-digit number.

If you are dividing 48 by 3, you might decide to split the number 48 into 30 (which is 10 × 3) and 18 (which is 6 × 3).

Breaking the number into chunks is quicker than counting 16 lots of 3 until you reach 48.

48 ÷ 3

48

30   **18**
(10 × 3)   (6 × 3)

Example

How many 5s are in 80?

80 can be chunked into 50 and 30.
10 x 5 = 50
6 x 5 = 30
10 + 6 = 16
So, 80 ÷ 5 = 16.

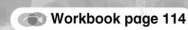
Lesson 1: **Multiplication and division facts (2)**

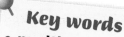

Key words
• **multiply**
• **times-tables**
• **divide**
• **multiple**

• Know multiplication facts up to 10 × 10 and the related division facts
• Recognise multiples of 2, 3, 4, 5 and 10

Discover

There are several strategies you can use to help remember multiplication facts.

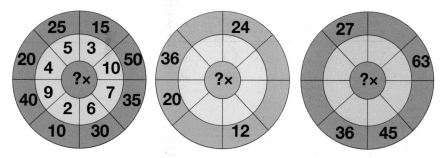

Learn

Multiplication facts are important to know.
Here are some ways to help recall them.

— If you know the patterns of a multiple, it can help you predict what the answer might look like. For example, multiples of 5 always end in a 5 or a 0.

What is 4 × 9?

> The digits in a multiple of 9 always add to 9 and multiples of 4 are every other even number. So 4 × 9 = 36 looks right.

— Multiplications make the same total if you swap the numbers around. If you know what 6 × 4 is, you also know what 4 × 6 is.

— You can use other times-tables facts to help. To find 6 × 8, you can first work out 5 × 8 and then add another 8.

What is the product of 9 and 6?

> I know that 10 sixes are 60, so if I take one lot of six away from 60, I will be left with 9 sixes. 60 − 6 = 54, so 9 × 6 = 54.

Lesson 2: **Doubling and halving (1)**

- Double 2-digit numbers, multiples of 10 to 500 and multiples of 100 to 5000
- Know corresponding halves

Key words
- double
- halve
- inverse
- multiple

Discover

Doubling and halving are **inverse** operations.

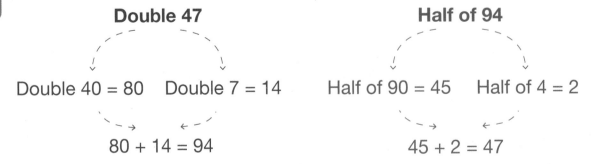

Double 47

Double 40 = 80   Double 7 = 14

80 + 14 = 94

Half of 94

Half of 90 = 45   Half of 4 = 2

45 + 2 = 47

Learn

One way to double a number quickly is to partition it into smaller numbers.

The number 68 can be partitioned into 60 and 8.

Double 60 is 120 and double 8 is 16, so double 68 is equal to the total of these two amounts. 120 + 16 = 136, so the answer is 136.

Halving is the inverse, or opposite, of this, so we can use this to check the answer is correct.

$$\text{Half of } 136 = (100 \div 2) + (30 \div 2) + (6 \div 2)$$
$$= 50 + 15 + 3$$
$$= 68$$

Example

What is double 75?

Double 75
$= (70 \times 2) + (5 \times 2)$
$= 140 + 10$
$= 150$

What number doubled equals 480?

Half of 480
$= (400 \div 2) + (80 \div 2)$
$= 200 + 40$
$= 240$

Lesson 3: **Multiplying and dividing by 10 (1)**

- Multiply and divide 3-digit numbers by 10

Key words
- multiply
- divide
- decimal point
- decimal
- value

Number

Discover

Multiplying and dividing a 3-digit number by 10 doesn't change the digits. Instead, the digits move to the left or the right.

 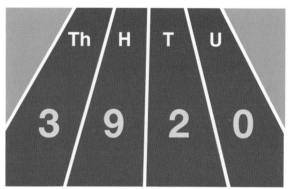

Learn

When a 3-digit number is multiplied by 10, its digits shift one place to the left just like the digits have changed lanes in the running track above.

You write a zero to show that there are no units.

When a 3-digit number is divided by 10, its digits shift one place to the right.

Example

What is 437 × 10?

Th	H	T	U	·	t
	4	3	7		
4	3	7	0		

437 × 10 = 4370

What is 437 ÷ 10?

Th	H	T	U	·	t
	4	3	7	·	
		4	3	·	7

437 ÷ 10 = 43.7

Lesson 4: **Multiplying and dividing by 10 (2)**

- Multiply and divide 3-digit numbers by 10

Discover

To multiply or divide a number by 10, you just need to shift all the digits to the left or right.

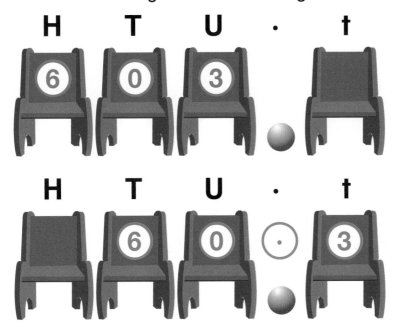

Learn

When 603 is divided by 10, the digits move one place to the right, just like the digits have shifted along the chairs in the picture above.

The units digit moves into the tenths place, so the number becomes a decimal.

Example

$782 \times 10 = 7820$

Th	H	T	U	.	t
	7	8	2		
7	8	2	0		

$525 \div 10 = 52{\cdot}5$

Th	H	T	U	.	t
	5	2	5		
		5	2	.	5

Lesson 5: **Multiplying a 2-digit number (3)**

- Multiply a 2-digit number by a single-digit number

Number

Discover

To multiply a 2-digit number by a single-digit number, it is helpful to partition the larger number.

Partitioning

$(50 \times 4) + (8 \times 4)$

 **58 × 4**

$= 200 + 32$

$= 232$

Grid method

×	50	8
4	200	32

$200 + 32 = 232$

Learn

The two written methods to multiply 2-digit by single-digit numbers that you have learned so far are very similar.

Although they look different, both of them involve partitioning the 2-digit number to make the calculation easier.

Example

What is 62×9?

Partitioning:

$62 \times 9 = (60 \times 9) + (2 \times 9)$

$\qquad = 540 + 18$

$\qquad = 558$

Grid method:

×	60	2
9	540	18

$540 + 18 = 558$

Lesson 6: **Multiplying a 2-digit number (4)**

- Multiply a 2-digit number by a single-digit number

Discover

When numbers are large, you can use written methods to help you to multiply them.

How many days?

15 weeks to go.

Learn

You know two different, but similar, ways to multiply 2-digit numbers by single-digit numbers. You can use which ever method you like best.

Both methods involve partitioning the 2-digit number. For example, 37 will become 30 and 7 and 86 will become 80 and 6.

Example

What is 37×4?

$37 \times 4 = (30 \times 4) + (7 \times 4)$

$\qquad = 120 + 28$

$\qquad = 148$

What is the product of 86 and 2?

$\times$	80	6
2	160	12

$160 + 12 = 172$

Lesson 7: **Dividing a 2-digit number (3)**

Key words
• **divide**
• **split**
• **inverse**

- Divide a 2-digit number by a single-digit number

Discover

Multiplication facts are helpful when dividing numbers.

Number of days:
‖‖ ‖‖ ‖‖ ‖‖ ‖‖ ‖‖
‖‖ ‖‖ ‖‖ ‖‖ ‖‖ ‖‖
‖‖ ‖‖ ‖‖ ‖‖ ‖‖‖‖
How many weeks?

12 weeks

Learn

One way to work out how many of a number fit into a larger number is to repeatedly subtract them away.

For example:

How many 5s are in 85?

85

$- 5 = 80$ (− 1 five)

$- 5 = 75$ (− 1 five)

$- 5 = 70$ (− 1 five)

$- 5 = 65$ ...and so on

A much quicker way is to split the number into larger chunks.

Example

What is $45 \div 3$?

$45 - 30 = 15$ (− 10 threes)

$15 - 15 = 0$ (− 5 threes)

$= 15$

Lesson 8: **Dividing a 2-digit number (4)**

- Divide a 2-digit number by a single-digit number
- Round up or down after division

Discover

Sometimes to answer a problem that involves division, you need to round the answer up or down.

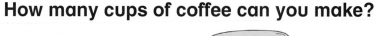

How many cups of coffee can you make?

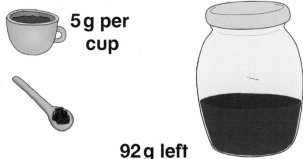

5 g per cup

92 g left

Learn

If there is a **remainder** to a division word problem, you often need to round the answer up or down to answer the problem correctly.

> ### Example
> **Note: the small 'r' stands for 'remainder'.**
> 99 chocolate bars need to be packed into boxes to be sent to the shops. How many full boxes can be sent?
> 99 − 60 = 39   (− 10 sixes)
> 39 − 36 = 3   (− 6 sixes)
>   = 16 r 3
> The answer should be rounded down to 16 boxes as the remaining 3 do not make a full box.
>
> 90 children are going on a school trip. Each minibus can take 8 children. How many minibuses will be needed?
> 90 − 80 = 10   (− 10 eights)
> 10 − 8 = 2   (− 1 eight)
>   = 11 r 2
> The answer should be rounded up to 12 minibuses as the remaining 2 children will need a minibus to travel in too!

Lesson 1: **Multiplication and division facts (3)**

- Know multiplication facts up to 10 × 10 and the related division facts

Number

Discover

Each times-tables fact that you learn can help with two different multiplication facts and two different division facts.

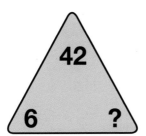
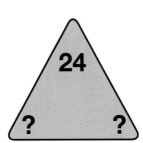

Learn

If you know one fact, it can help with many more.

If you know that 4 × 5 = 20, you also know that 5 × 4 = 20 because multiplications are the same both ways.

Division is the inverse of multiplication, so you also know that 20 ÷ 5 = 4 and 20 ÷ 4 = 5.

You can also use facts to help with other times-tables. You can use 4 × 5 = 20 to find 4 × 4 (one less 4), 4 × 6 (one more 4), 4 × 10 (double 20).

Example

7 × 8 = 56

So,   8 × 7 = 56   56 ÷ 8 = 7   56 ÷ 7 = 8

        7 × 7 = 56 − 7 = 49   7 × 9 = 56 + 7 = 63

and so on.

Lesson 2: **Doubling and halving (2)**

Key words
* double
* halve
* inverse
* multiple

* Double 2-digit numbers, multiples of 10 to 500 and multiples of 100 to 5000
* Know the corresponding halves

Number

Discover

Doubling and halving are opposites, so you can use halving to check that you have doubled a number correctly.

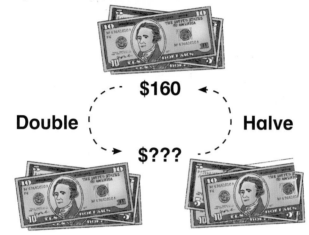

Learn

Once you know how to double 2-digit numbers, you can use this information to double multiples of 10 and 100.

For example, double 45 equals 90. So, double 450 equals 900 and double 4500 equals 9000.

You can halve 2-digit numbers by dividing by two.

Use your knowledge of the x 2 multiplication and division facts and partitioning.

Example

What is 680 doubled?	What is 680 halved?
Double 68 = (60 × 2) + (8 × 2)	Half 68 = (60 ÷ 2) + (8 ÷ 2)
= 120 + 16	= 30 + 4
= 136	= 34
So double 680 is 1360.	So half 680 is 340.

Lesson 3: **Multiplying a 2-digit number (5)**

- Multiply a 2-digit number by a single-digit number

Key words
- partition
- grid method
- total
- altogether
- product

Discover

You can use the strategy of partitioning numbers or the grid method to help with everyday calculations.

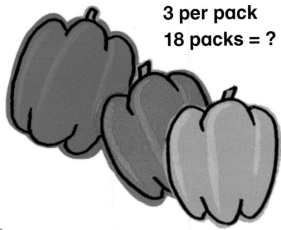

3 per pack
18 packs = ?

Learn

Real-life problems do not say which operation is needed to solve them. Instead, they contain clues that point to how to answer them.

If the clues point towards multiplication, you can answer the question mentally, or by using partitioning or the grid method.

Once you have completed the calculation, use the answer to solve the word problem by writing a short phrase or sentence.

Example

There are five chocolate bars in a pack.
How many chocolate bars are in 26 packs?

×	20	6
5	100	30

100 + 30 = 130
There are 130 chocolate bars.

Number

Lesson 4: **Dividing a 2-digit number (5)**

• Divide a 2-digit number by a single-digit number

Discover

Not every division question ends in a whole number – sometimes there is a remainder.

Children must work in groups of 5. There are 31 children in the class. How many groups of 5?

Learn

Knowing your times-tables facts is an important skill to help divide 2-digit numbers by single-digit numbers.

You can partition the number into known multiples.

If there is a remainder, you can then decide whether to keep it, or to round it up or down, depending on the problem.

Example

Oranges are sold in bags of six. There are 82 oranges ready to be packed. How many full bags can be made?

82
− 60 = 22 (subtract 10 sixes)
− 18 = 4 (subtract 3 sixes)
     = 13 remainder 4

The 4 remaining oranges aren't enough to fill a bag, so the answer needs to be rounded down to 13 bags.

Lesson 5: **Multiplying and dividing 2-digit numbers**

- Multiply and divide a 2-digit number by a single-digit number

Key words
- multiplication
- division
- operation
- per

Discover

Word problems contain all the information needed to choose the correct operation and then answer the question.

Ryan reads ⑦② pages over ⑥ days. He reads the <u>same number</u> of pages <u>every day</u>. <u>How many pages</u> does he read <u>each day</u>?

He reades 12 pages a day

Learn

Real-life problems don't tell you which operation to use. Think about the problem carefully and identify any key words or phrases that might act as clues.

Once you know the operation, you can work out the answer.

Example

At the market there are 7 boxes of oranges. There are 15 oranges in each box. How many oranges are there altogether?

The important information in this word problem are the numbers 15 and 7 and the words 'in each', 'How many' and 'altogether'.

It is describing 7 groups of 15, so the operation to use is multiplication.

$$15 \times 7 = (10 \times 7) + (5 \times 7)$$
$$= 70 + 35$$
$$= 105 \text{ oranges}$$

Lesson 6: **Ratio and proportion (1)**

- Understand and write simple statements about proportion

Discover

These animals are not in proportion. When a shape, picture or object is in proportion it means that their relative sizes are the same.

Learn

Have you ever drawn a picture of someone and had to start again because their head looked too big compared to their body?

This means you are already beginning to understand about **proportion**. Proportion can be used to compare amounts such as height and mass.

For example, you might say that you are twice as tall as your sister or that an office block is $\frac{1}{3}$ of the height of the one next to it.

Example

The first row of cubes is $\frac{1}{2}$ as long as the second.

The second row of cubes is double the length of the first.

Lesson 7: **Ratio and proportion (2)**

- Use simple fractions to show and work out proportion

Number

Discover

Often proportion is used to show the size something is in real life.

$\frac{1}{4}$ **actual width**

Learn

You can use fractions to compare one thing with another. For example, the photograph is $\frac{1}{4}$ of the width of the real flower. If the flower in the photograph is 3 cm wide, the real flower would be 4×3 cm wide.

Example

A model car is $\frac{1}{3}$ of the actual length of a real car.

The model is 1 m long.

How long is the car in real life?

1 m

If the model is $\frac{1}{3}$ of the actual length, the actual size must be three times as large. 3×1 m = 3 m, so the car must be 3 m long in real life.

Lesson 8: **Ratio and proportion (3)**

Key words
• fraction
• ratio
• compare

• Begin to understand and use ratio to describe simple relationships

Discover

A **ratio** is used to state how much of one thing there is compared to something else.

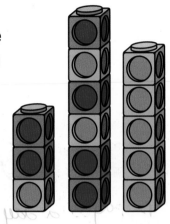

Learn

You can compare part of something to another part.
In this row of cubes, there are 2 green cubes for every 3 purple cubes. The ratio is 2 : 3.
You say, 'The **ratio** is two to three.'

You can also compare part of something to the whole.
There are 2 green cubes out of a total of 5 cubes altogether.
$\frac{2}{5}$ of the whole row is green.

Example

There are 4 boys and 2 girls in a group.
What is the ratio of girls to boys in the group?

There are 2 girls and 4 boys, so the ratio is 2 girls for every 4 boys, or 2 to 4 (2 : 4).

What fraction of the group are boys?

There are six children in the group altogether, so the number of boys is 4 out of 6, which is $\frac{4}{6}$.

Lesson 1: **Different polygons**

- Identify, describe, visualise, draw and classify a variety of 2D shapes and find real-life examples of them

Discover

What can you learn about these heptagons?
Are they regular or irregular?

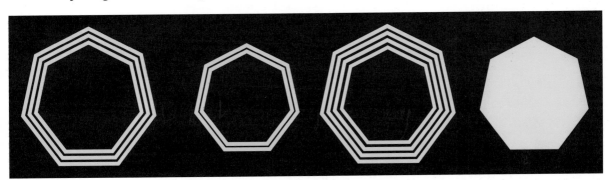

Geometry

Learn

A heptagon has seven sides and seven vertices.

A regular heptagon

An irregular heptagon

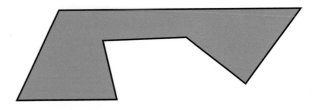

A **quadrilateral** is the name of any shape with four sides and four vertices.

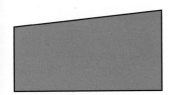

73

Lesson 2: **Quadrilaterals**

- Identify, describe, visualise, draw and classify a variety of quadrilaterals and find real-life examples of them

Key words
- quadrilateral
- parallelogram
- rectangle
- square
- rhombus
- kite
- trapezium

Discover

Learn

A square is the only regular quadrilateral. A square is also a rectangle. A rectangle has four sides and four right angles.

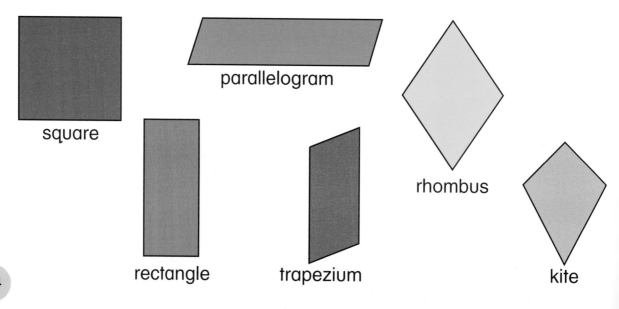

square

parallelogram

rectangle

trapezium

rhombus

kite

Lesson 3: **Classifying polygons**

Key words
• polygon
• quadrilateral
• heptagon
• symmetry
• right angle
• classify

• Identify, describe, visualise and draw a variety of polygons and classify them

Discover

Learn

There are many different ways to classify polygons. These include:

• whether or not they are regular
• number of sides or vertices
• number of parallel sides
• whether or not they have right angles
• if they are symmetrical.

Example

Look at how these shapes have been classified.

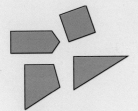   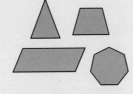

Right angles   **No right angles**

Lesson 4: **Drawing polygons**

- Identify, describe, visualise and draw a variety of polygons
- Identify 2D shapes in drawings and pictures

Key words
- polygon
- quadrilateral
- heptagon
- symmetry
- right angle

Discover

This building has different 2D shapes in the windows. How many can you see?

Learn

If you know the properties of regular polygons, you can make accurate drawings of them using rulers and square or dot grid paper.

Example

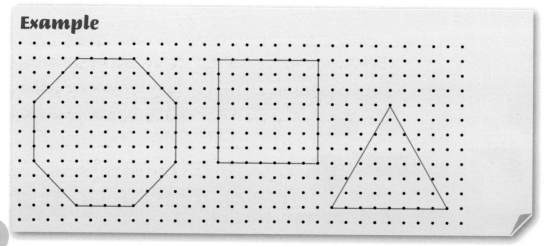

Lesson 5: **Identifying lines of symmetry**

- polygon
- line of symmetry
- regular shape
- irregular shape

- Identify lines of symmetry in 2D shapes and in the environment

Discover

What lines of symmetry can you see on the building?

Geometry

Learn

If something is symmetrical, one half will be the same as the other half. A shape can have more than one line of symmetry.

Example

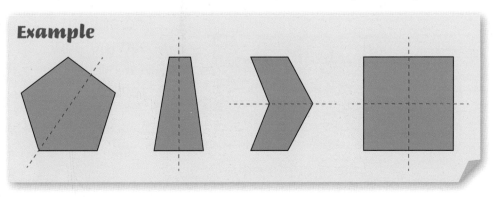

77

Lesson 6: **Completing symmetrical figures and patterns**

> **Key words**
> • line of symmetry
> • symmetrical
> • mirror line

• Complete symmetrical figures and patterns

Discover

This is the flag of Thailand. What lines of symmetry can you see?

Learn

A mirror can help you to make patterns and figures symmetrical. You place the mirror on the line of symmetry and draw what you can see on the other side of the line.

Example

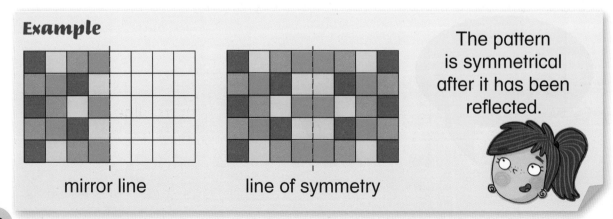

mirror line   line of symmetry

The pattern is symmetrical after it has been reflected.

Lesson 7: **Reflecting along a line of symmetry**

Key words
• line of symmetry
• mirror line

• Reflect 2D shapes and patterns along a line of symmetry

Discover

This is the city of Hong Kong. What reflections can you see?

Learn

A reflection is a shape or an image seen as it would be in a mirror. A mirror helps you to make shapes or images symmetrical and also to draw reflections.

Example

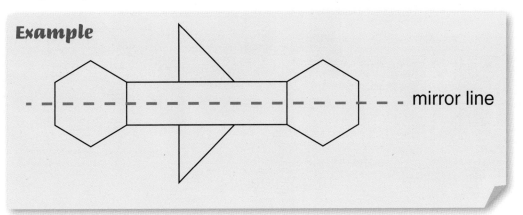

mirror line

Lesson 8: **Repeated reflection to make patterns**

Key words
• line of symmetry
• mirror line

• Repeatedly reflect 2D shapes and patterns along a line of symmetry

Discover

Learn

A shape can be repeatedly reflected through lines of symmetry to create a pattern. This will make a sequence where every odd numbered shape and every even numbered shape will be the same.

Example

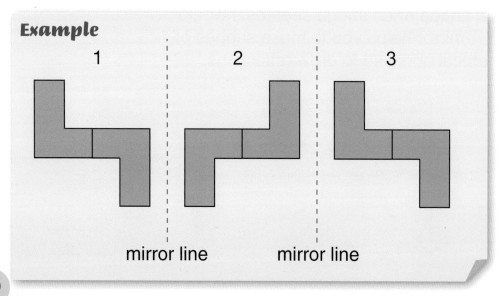

1   2   3

mirror line   mirror line

80

Geometry

Lesson 1: **Identifying 3D shapes**

Key words
- polyhedron
- polyhedra
- prism
- pyramid
- vertices
- apex

- Identify and describe a range of 3D shapes
- Identify similarities and differences between 3D shapes

Discover

What 3D shapes can you see in this picture?
One is a non-polyhedron. Which one is it?

Learn

You can identify 3D shapes by looking at their properties.

These include the number and shape of faces, number of edges and vertices, if they have them.

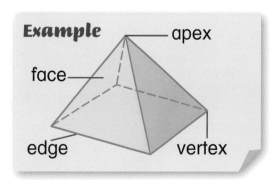

Example — apex

face —

edge   vertex

Geometry

Lesson 2: **Recognising 3D shapes**

Key words
- polyhedron
- polyhedra
- prism
- pyramid
- vertices
- apex

• Recognise a wider range of 3D shapes in different orientations

Geometry

Discover

Look at these shapes. How many can you identify? Which of these are polyhedra? How do you know?

Learn

You can identify 3D shapes from their properties, regardless of their orientation. A cube has 6 square faces, 12 edges and 8 vertices. It does not matter which position it is in, it will always be a cube.

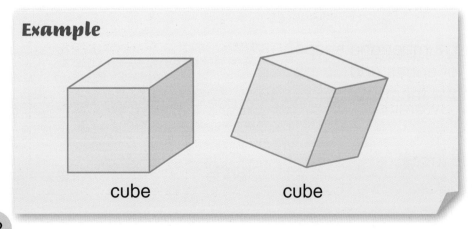

Example

cube   cube

Lesson 3: **Classifying 3D shapes**

Key words
- polyhedron
- non-polyhedron
- classify
- prism
- pyramid
- vertices

• Classify a range of different 3D shapes

Discover
Look at the polyhedra in the picture.

Geometry

Learn
There are different ways to classify 3D shapes. These include:
• whether they are polyhedra
• whether they are prisms
• whether they are pyramids
• the number of faces
• the shapes of the faces
• the number of edges
• the number of vertices.

Example
Look at how these shapes have been classified.

Prisms	Not prisms

83

Lesson 4: **Nets**

- Visualise 3D objects from 2D nets and make nets of 3D shapes

Discover

What shape do you think one of these would be if it was opened up?

Learn

You can make 3D shapes from nets. Here are some examples of nets that make cubes and cuboids.

Example
cubes

cuboids

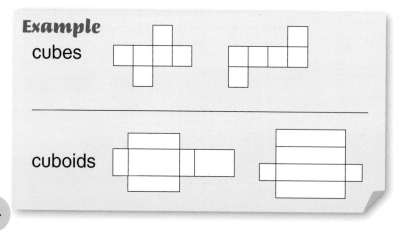

84

Lesson 1: **Recognising and describing position**

• Describe and identify positions on a grid

Discover

What do you recognise on this map of a zoo?

Learn

You can identify the position of things on a co-ordinate grid by saying the number on the horizontal axis first, then the number in the vertical axis. These can be between the lines as on the map above, or on the lines as on the grid below.

Example

The centre of the triangle is positioned at (6, 5).

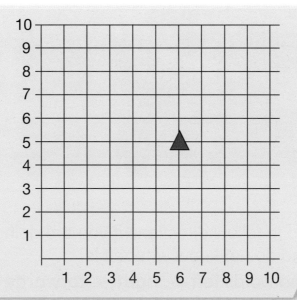

Geometry

85

Lesson 2: **Recognising and describing directions**

- Give directions to follow a given path

Discover

What do you think this signpost shows you?
What clues are there that will help you find out?

Learn

You often need to follow directions if you are going somewhere and do not know where it is.

You can use the words **left ←**, **right →**, **forwards ↑** and **backwards ↓**.

Lesson 3: **Angles**

- Know that angles are measured in degrees
- Know that one whole turn is 360° which is equal to four right angles

Key words
- **degrees**
- **turn**
- **right angle**
- **perpendicular**

Geometry

Discover

Learn

A right angle measures 90°.

A straight line is made from two right angles and measures 180°.

Three right angles measure 270°.

A whole turn is made from four right angles and measures 360°.

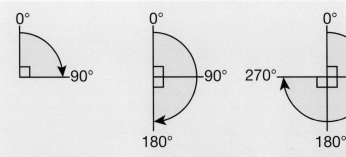

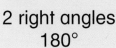

1 right angle
90°

2 right angles
180°

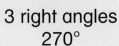

3 right angles
270°

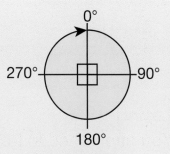

4 right angles
360°

87

Lesson 4: **Comparing and ordering angles**

- Compare and order angles less than 180°

Discover

Can you see a right angle?
Can you see angles that are less than,
or greater than, a right angle?

Learn

You can compare angles using a set square. It will help you find
angles that are greater and less than a right angle.

Example

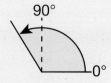

Less than a right angle (acute)   Right angle   Greater than a right angle (obtuse)

Geometry

88

Lesson 1: **Units of Length**

- Choose and use units to measure length
- Record length in mm, cm, m and km

Key words
- **kilometre (km)**
- **metre (m)**
- **centimetre (cm)**
- **millimetre (mm)**
- **length**
- **distance**

Discover

Learn

There are 10 mm in 1 cm.

There are 100 cm in 1 m.

There are 1000 m in 1 km.

There are 5 mm in $\frac{1}{2}$ cm.

There are 25 cm in $\frac{1}{4}$ m.

There are 750 m in $\frac{3}{4}$ km.

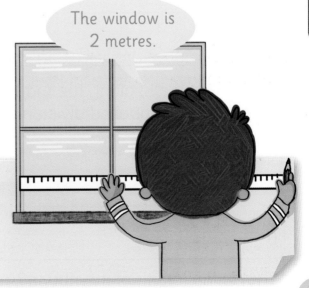

The window is 2 metres.

When you measure something you need to choose the unit to use – millimetres, centimetres, metres or kilometres.

Measure

Lesson 2: **Reading and interpreting length**

- Read and show length on a ruler or metre stick that is only partially numbered

Key words
- metre (m)
- centimetre (cm)
- millimetre (mm)
- number line

Discover

Learn

The paintbrush is nearly 20 cm long. You can count back along the marks to find how many centimetres long it is exactly.

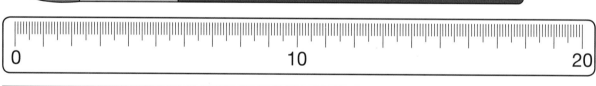

```
0                    10                    20
```

```
20   21   22   23   24   25   26   27   28   29   30
```

Count on, or back, along the marks on a ruler from the nearest multiple of 10 or labelled division to find the missing numbers.

Example

```
0                    10          16 17 18 19 20
```

What is the length of the ribbon?   16 cm

Measure

Lesson 3: **Estimating, measuring and recording length**

* Estimate length and distances
* Record length in metres and centimetres

Discover

Measure

Learn

Knowing what 1 cm and 5 cm look like helps us estimate length in centimetres.

___
1 cm

_____
5 cm

Example

Estimate and measure the lengths of lines A, B and C.

I estimate that line A is 6 cm long. I can use a ruler to measure the actual length of the line.

A _____   B _____   C _____

Lesson 4: **Problems involving length**

• Solve word problems involving length

Discover

So far these walkers have walked a third of the distance to the camp site. We can work out how far they have walked in metres, by using the information we can see and remembering facts about measuring length.

Learn

To solve problems involving length and distance, use the information in the question and decide whether it is an addition, subtraction, multiplication or division problem.

Remember these facts to help you:

1 km = 1000 m
1 m = 100 cm
1 cm = 10 mm

Example

Lola runs 1 km on Monday, 3 km on Wednesday and 2 km on Thursday. How many metres has she run this week?

1 km + 3 km + 2 km = 6 km
1 km in m = 1000 m
6 × 1000 m = 6000 m
The answer is 6000 m.

Measure

Lesson 1: **Units of mass**

- Choose and use units to measure mass
- Understand the relationship between g and kg

Key words
- **kilogram (kg)**
- **gram (kg)**
- **mass**
- **weight**

Discover

This person is measuring her weight in kilograms (kg).

Learn

There are 1000 grams in 1 kilogram.
There are 500 grams in half a kilogram.
There are 250 grams in a quarter of a kilogram.

Example
What is the mass of the scissors?   40 g

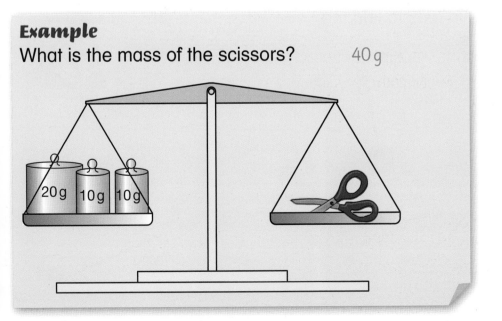

Measure

93

Lesson 2: **Reading and interpreting mass**

- Read and show mass on a scale that is only partially numbered

Discover

Learn

Divide each section into 10 and count along the marks in tens to find the missing numbers.

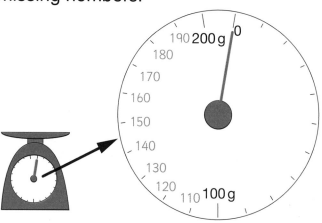

Example
What is the mass shown on the scales?

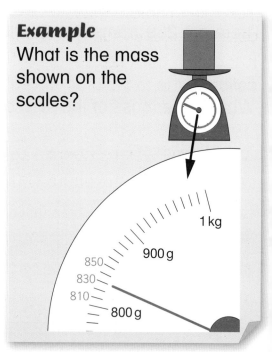

94

Lesson 3: **Estimating, measuring and recording mass**

- Estimate mass
- Record mass in grams and kilograms

Discover

Learn

You can estimate mass by thinking about how heavy an object feels compared to something else.

Knowing what 1 kg, 10 g and 100 g feel like can help us to estimate the mass of an object.

Measure

Example

Which fruit weighs about 1 kg?
Which fruit weighs about 100 g?

The pineapple is the heaviest.

95

Lesson 4: **Problems involving mass**

• Solve word problems involving mass

Discover

Each apple weighs about 150 g. We can work out how much the bag of 5 apples weighs by calculating 5 × 150 g.

Learn

To solve problems involving mass, use the information in the question and decide whether it is an addition, subtraction, multiplication or division problem.

Remember this fact to help you:

1000 g = kg

Example

Six children each have 50 g of peas on their plates. How much would all the peas weigh together?

6 × 50 g = 300 g

The answer is 300 g.

Measure

Lesson 1: **Units of capacity**

- Choose and use units to measure capacity
- Understand the relationship between ml and l

Discover

This girl is measuring milk in millilitres.
Millilitres are used to measure small amounts of liquids.
To measure larger amounts of liquid, you use litres.

Learn

litres = l

millilitres = ml

There are 1000 millilitres in a litre.

There are 500 millilitres in half a litre.

There are 250 millilitres in one quarter of a litre.

There are 750 millilitres in three quarters of a litre.

Measure

Example

How much is 5 litres in mililitres?

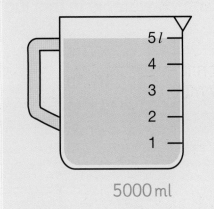

5000 ml

97

Lesson 2: **Reading and interpreting capacity**

- Read and show capacity on a scale that is only partially numbered

Discover

There is 36 ml of liquid in this container.

Measure

Learn

These facts can help you to find measurements ending in 50, 25 or 75.

Half of 100 is 50.

Half of 50 is 25.

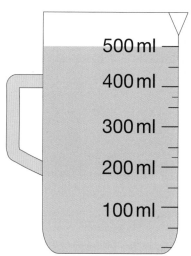

Example

How much water is in this jug?

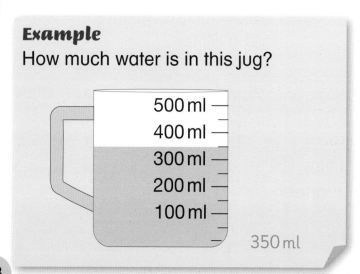

350 ml

Lesson 3: **Estimating, measuring and recording capacity**

* Estimate capacity and record it in litres and millilitres

Key words
* **litre (_l_)**
* **millilitre (ml)**
* **capacity**
* **estimate**

Discover

Knowing what 100 ml looks like can help you estimate amounts of liquid.

Learn

100 ml of liquid looks different in containers of different sizes and shapes.

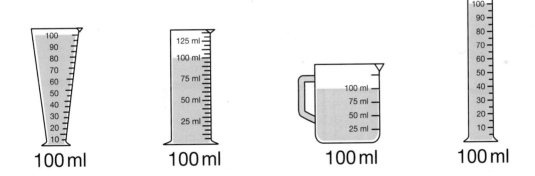

100 ml   100 ml   100 ml   100 ml

Measure

Example

Match the containers to their estimated capacity.

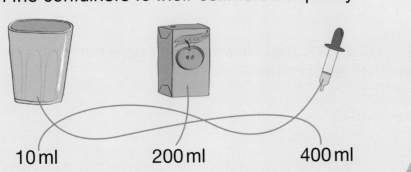

10 ml   200 ml   400 ml

Workbook page 200

Lesson 4: **Problems involving capacity**

• Solve word problems involving capacity

Discover

Learn

To solve problems involving capacity, use the information in the question and decide whether it is an addition, subtraction, multiplication or division problem.

Remember this fact to help you:

1000 ml = 1 litre

Example

There is 400 ml of water in a jug. How many people can each have 50 ml of water from the jug?

400 divided by 50 = 8

8 x 50 = 400

The answer is 8.

Measure

Lesson 1: **Revising length**

- Estimate and measure length in metres and centimetres
- Record length using decimal notation

Key words
- kilometre (km)
- metre (m)
- centimetre (cm)
- millimetre (mm)
- length
- height

Discover

0·7 m is the same as 70 cm.

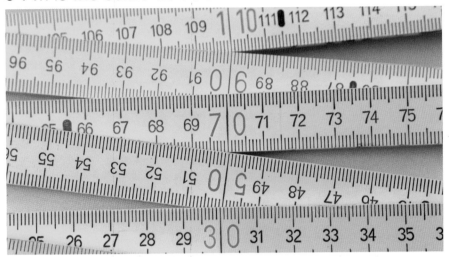

Learn

1 metre is 100 centimetres long. Every 10 cm is 0·1 of a metre.

10 cm = 0·1 m   20 cm = 0·2 m

If the number of centimetres is not a multiple of 10 (for example, 67 cm), it is written like this: 0·67 m

The decimal point separates metres from centimetres:

4 m 82 cm = 4·82 m

Example

How long is the pencil? Give the answer using decimal notation.

0·25 m

Measure

101

Lesson 2: **Revising mass**

- Estimate and measure mass in grams and kilograms
- Record mass using decimal notation

Discover

The customer wants 1·5 kg of apples.

Learn

1 kilogram is made up of 1000 grams. Every 100 g is 0·1 of a kilogram.

100 g = 0·1 kg   200 g = 0·2 kg

If the number of grams is not a multiple of 100 for example, 34 g, it is written like this: 0·34 kg.

The decimal point separates kilograms from grams: 6 kg 500 g = 6·5 g.

Example

What are the masses shown on the scales in kilograms and grams?

Lesson 3: **Revising capacity**

- Estimate and measure capacity in litres and millilitres
- Record capacity using decimal notation

Discover

0·3*l*

Learn

1 litre is 1000 millilitres.

Every 100 ml is 0·1 of a litre.

500 ml = 0·5 *l*   600 ml = 0·6 *l*

If the number of millilitres is not a multiple of 100 (for example, 620), it is written 0·62 *l*.

The decimal point separates litres from millilitres:

3 *l* 450 ml = 3·45 *l*.

Measure

Example

What is the capacity of the petrol can in litres and millilitres?

4·3 *l*

4300 ml

The capacity is 4 litres 300 millilitres.

Lesson 4: **Problems involving measures**

- Solve word problems involving measures
- Record measures using decimal notation

Key words
- **kilometre (km)**
- **metre (m)**
- **centimetre (cm)**
- **kilogram (kg)**
- **gram (g)**
- **litre (*l*)**
- **millilitre (ml)**

Discover

Learn

To solve measures problems involving decimals.

1 Look carefully to make sure all measures are written in the same unit. If necessary, convert all measures to the same unit.

2 Work out whether it is an addition, subtraction, multiplication or division problem.

3 Work out the answer. If necessary, convert the answer to a different unit of measure.

These facts about measures might help you.

150 cm = 1·5 m   1750 m = 1·75 km

1250 g = 1·25 kg   1100 ml = 1·1 litre

Example

A snail travelled 12 cm to the north, 4 cm to the west, then 8 cm east. How many metres has the snail travelled altogether?

12 cm + 4 cm + 8 cm = 24 cm

0·24 m

Measure

Lesson 1: **Telling the time on an analogue clock**

- Read and tell time to the nearest minute on an analogue clock
- Use a.m. and p.m.

> **Key words**
> - minute
> - hour
> - analogue clock
> - 12-hour time
> - a.m.
> - p.m.

Discover

Learn

To tell the time to the nearest minute, you focus on the minutes past the hour. If the minute hand is one minute past the 7, you know that it is 36 minutes past. You can count in 5s and know that the 7 shows 35 minutes past. One more minute is 36 minutes past.

Example

This time reads 36 minutes past 10. It also reads 24 minutes to 11.

Measure

105

Lesson 2: **Telling the time on a digital clock**

- Tell the time correctly to one minute on analogue and digital clocks

Discover

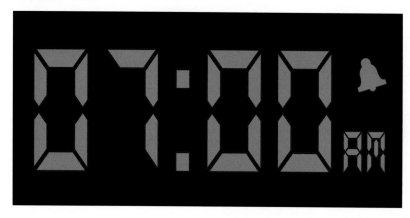

Learn

Times are shown on analogue clocks with numbers and hands.

On digital clocks, times are shown with numbers and a symbol to separate the hours and minutes.

Example

14 minutes past 8 in the evening.

42 minutes past 5 in the morning is the same as 18 minutes to 6 in the morning.

Measure

Lesson 3: **Timetables and calendars**

- Read a calendar and timetable and work out time intervals

Discover

Learn

Calendars show the dates during the year.
They are arranged into months, weeks and days.

Timetables are useful to plan our time, such as when we need to catch a bus.

Measure

Example

The timetable shows when the bus travels between the villages.

Bus stop	Arrival time		
Market Street	10:15	10:35	10:55
Northford	10:25	10:45	11:05
Easton	10:35	10:55	11:15
Southam	10:45	11:05	11:25
Westerby	10:55	11:15	11:35

Lesson 4: **Measuring time intervals**

- Choose units of time to measure time intervals

Discover

Can you think of any sports where people race like this?
How do they work out how fast they ran?

Learn

We can find time differences if we know the start and finish times.

Using a number line to find the differences is helpful.

Example

A plane departs at 3:15 p.m. and lands at 5:55 p.m.
How long was the flight?

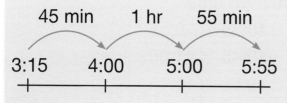

45 min   1 hr   55 min

3:15   4:00   5:00   5:55

The flight was 2 hr 40 min.

Measure

Lesson 1: **Perimeter (1)**

• Draw rectangles to specific measurements
• Measure and calculate their perimeters

Key words
• perimeter
• distance
• centimetre (cm)
• length
• width

Discover

Learn

Perimeter is the distance around the outside of a shape or space.

You can find the perimeter of a shape by measuring each side and finding the total.

Example
The perimeter of this rectangle is:

6 cm + 2 cm + 6 cm + 2 cm = 16 cm

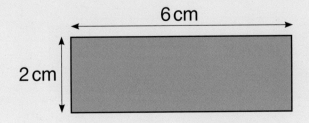

6 cm

2 cm

Measure

109

Lesson 2: **Perimeter (2)**

- Draw rectangles to specific measurements
- Measure and calculate their perimeters

Discover

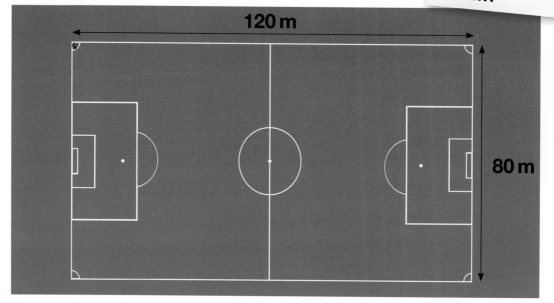

120 m

80 m

Learn

You can find the perimeter of any rectangle by adding the lengths of all four sides.

You could do this more quickly by adding the width and length, then doubling.

Example

The perimeter of this rectangle is double 7 cm + 2 cm, which is 9 cm × 2 = 18 cm.

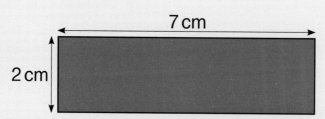

7 cm

2 cm

Measure

Lesson 3: **Area (1)**

• Understand that area is measured in square units and find the area of rectangles

Discover

Learn

A space like the one in the picture above is called an **area**.

An area is any amount of space inside a perimeter.

An area is the amount of space a shape covers.

Area is measured in square units, for example, square centimetres (cm²) or square metres (m²).

Example
The area of this rectangle is
20 square centimetres (20 cm²).
Its perimeter is 18 cm.

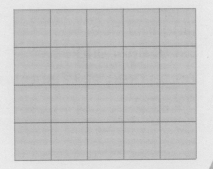

Measure

Lesson 4: **Area (2)**

• Understand that area is measured in square units and find the area of rectilinear shapes

Discover

What do you think this picture shows?
What shapes can you see?

Learn

You now know how to find the area of rectangles.
You can use this knowledge to help you to find the area of similar shapes. These shapes are called **rectilinear shapes**.

Example

This is a rectilinear shape.
The sides meet at right angles.

This shape has an area of 12 square centimetres (12 cm²).

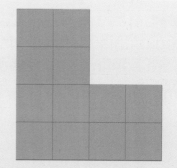

Measure

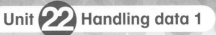
Lesson 1: **Tables, diagrams, tally charts and frequency tables**

> **Key words**
> * data
> * tables
> * tally
> * frequency table
> * diagrams

* Collect and sort information using tally charts and frequency tables

Discover

Learn

Data means information.

Handling data means collecting, sorting, and representing information.

Tables, diagrams, tally charts and frequency tables are useful tools for collecting information.

Tally charts record results using marks, frequency tables use numbers.

> ### Example
> This tally chart and frequency table shows the colour of sports tops worn by Class 4.
>
> | Shirt | Tally | Frequency |
> |-------|-------|-----------|
> | | ||| | 3 |
> | | �繁I | 6 |
> | | ᴺᴺ | 5 |
> | | | | 1 |

Handling data

113

Lesson 2: **Venn and Carroll diagrams**

Key words
• Venn diagram
• Carroll diagram
• sorting rule
• category
• region

• Use Venn and Carroll diagrams with two and three categories to organise information or objects

Discover

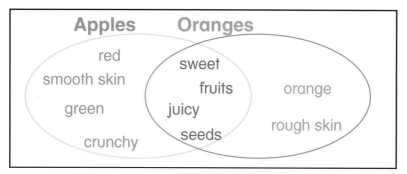

Learn

A Venn diagram compares and contrasts data. When drawing a Venn diagram, begin by considering what is the same about each of the sets. A Carroll diagram shows what fits and what does not fit, with no overlapping information and none outside the table.

Example

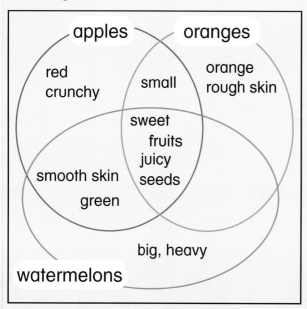

	Has brown eyes	Does not have brown eyes
Is shorter than 120 cm	Sundus Hamzah Nandini	James Tilly
Is 120 cm or taller	Rav Osman Farrah Babita	Rhoda Justin Kyle

Handling data

Lesson 3: **Pictograms (1)**

Key words
- **pictogram**
- **key**
- **symbols**
- **quantity**
- **scale**

- Construct and read pictograms with quantities of 2, 5, 10 or 20 represented by one picture

Discover

Pictogram to show numbers of bicycles sold in one week

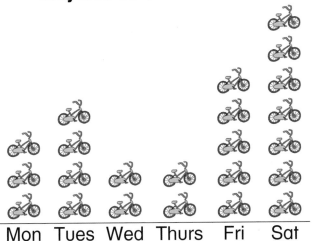

Key: 🚲 = 10 bicycles

Mon   Tues   Wed   Thurs   Fri   Sat

Learn

Pictograms are used to organise information.
The symbol represents the numerical information
and equals the number in the key.

Example

A library wanted to find out how many people used the
library each day. The pictogram shows the results.

People who used the library this week	
Mon	�
Tues	♦♦♦♦♦
Wed	♦♦♦♦♦
Thurs	♦♦♦♦♦♦
Fri	♦♦♦♦♦♦♦
Sat	♦♦♦♦♦♦♦♦
Sun	

Key: ♦ = 5 people

Handling data

115

Lesson 4: **Bar charts (1)**

• Construct and read bar charts with intervals of 2, 5, 10 or 20 on the vertical scale

Key words
• title
• horizontal axis
• vertical axis
• scale
• interval
• bar chart

Discover
Sale of breads in bakery

Breads	Total
flatbread	40
yeast bread	10
chappati	10
cornbread	30
rice pancakes	10

Learn

The bars in a bar chart show independent numbers and do not touch. They can be horizontal or vertical.

The greatest frequency determines the extent of the scale.

Example

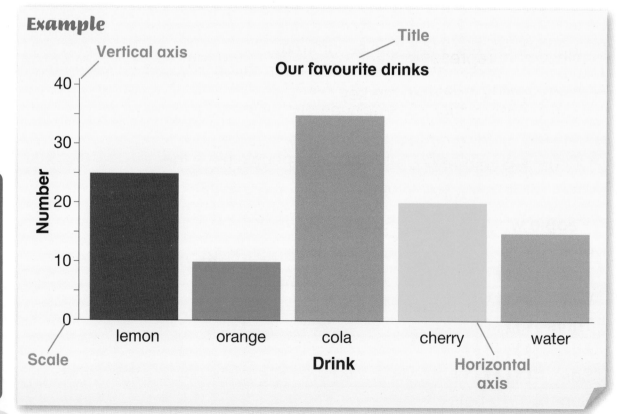

Handling data

Lesson 1: **Pictograms (2)**

• Read pictograms with whole and half symbols

Key words
• key
• symbol
• whole
• half

Discover

What's in the bag of sweets?

green	● ● ● ◖
orange	● ● ● ●
blue	● ● ◖
pink	● ● ●
yellow	● ● ● ● ● ◖
red	● ● ● ●
purple	● ● ● ◖
brown	● ◖

Key: ● = 2 sweets

Learn

A half symbol represents half the quantity of the key.

When choosing which symbol to use for a pictogram choose a symbol that can easily be divided in half.

A half symbol for a quantity of 5 has no meaning, because you cannot have $2\frac{1}{2}$ cats, or $2\frac{1}{2}$ people.

Example

Our pets

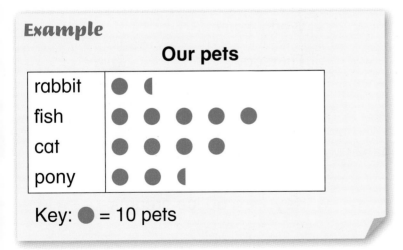

rabbit	● ◖
fish	● ● ● ● ●
cat	● ● ● ●
pony	● ● ◖

Key: ● = 10 pets

Handling data

Lesson 2: **Pictograms (3)**

• Read and construct pictograms where the symbol represents different units

Discover

Key: $ = 1

Money raised

Shaan	$ $ $ $ $ $ $ $ $
Daniel	$ $
Eva	$ $ $ $ $ $ $ $ $ $ $ $ $ $ $ $ $ $ $
Prisha	$ $ $ $ $ $ $ $ $ $ $ $ $ $

The same data could be represented with a different key.

Learn

Using symbols representing different units changes the look of a pictogram. You need to decide which key is best to use.

These pictograms both show the number of ice creams sold in a week. Which scale best represents the data?

Monday	𝅭 𝅭 𝅭 𝅭 𝅭
Tuesday	𝅭 𝅭 𝅭
Wednesday	𝅭 𝅭 𝅭
Thursday	𝅭 𝅭 𝅭 𝅭 𝅭
Friday	𝅭 𝅭 𝅭 𝅭 𝅭 𝅭 𝅭 𝅭
Saturday	𝅭 𝅭 𝅭 𝅭 𝅭 𝅭 𝅭 𝅭 𝅭 𝅭 𝅭 𝅭
Sunday	𝅭 𝅭 𝅭 𝅭 𝅭 𝅭 𝅭 𝅭 𝅭 𝅭 𝅭 𝅭 𝅭 𝅭 𝅭 𝅭 𝅭

Key: 𝅭 = 10 ice creams

Monday	𝅭
Tuesday	𝅭
Wednesday	𝅭
Thursday	𝅭
Friday	𝅭 𝅭
Saturday	𝅭 𝅭
Sunday	𝅭 𝅭 𝅭

Key: 𝅭 = 50 ice creams

Handling data

Lesson 3: **Bar charts (2)**

• Read and construct bar charts

Discover

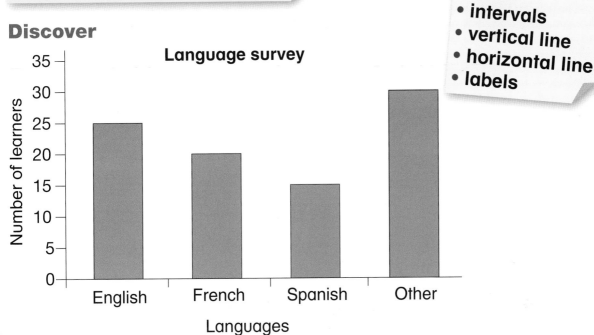

Language survey

Learn

In a bar chart, the frequency of the data is represented by the height or length of the bar. The height of the bars depends on the scale being used.

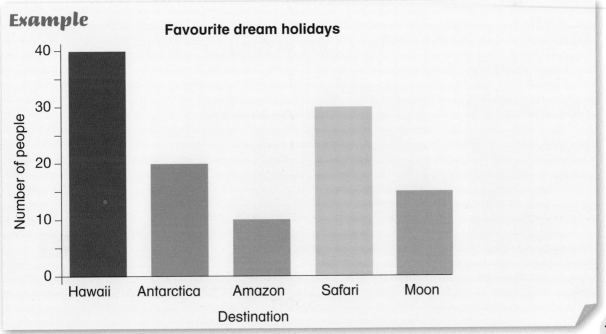

Example Favourite dream holidays

Handling data

Lesson 4: **Bar charts (3)**

- Read bar charts, interpreting frequencies between two labelled divisions

Key words
- scale
- intervals
- divisions
- vertical line
- horizontal line

Discover

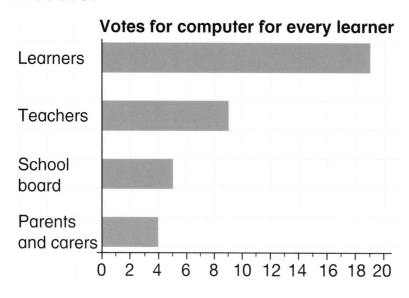

Votes for computer for every learner

Learn

To read between numbered scales, look to see which interval the scales goes up in, such as 2s, 10s or 20s. Read the marked numbers above and below to work out the frequency.

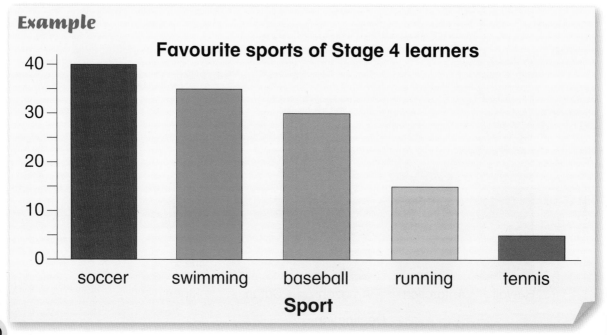

Example

Favourite sports of Stage 4 learners

Notes

Notes

Notes

Notes